Saints in transit

Saints
in transit

by
Frank Allred

GRACE PUBLICATIONS TRUST
7 Arlington Way
London EC1R 1XA
England
e-mail: editors@gracepublications.co.uk
www.gracepublications.co.uk

Managing Editors:
M. J. Adams
D. Crisp

First published 2010

ISBN 10: 0-946462-80-1   ISBN 13: 978-0-946462-80-3

Distributed by
EP BOOKS
Faverdale North
Darlington DL3 OPH
England

e-mail: sales@epbooks.org
www.epbooks.org

Printed and bound in UK by J F Print Ltd., Sparkford, Somerset.

Contents

Part One

What is a saint?

1. Becoming what we are

When is a saint a saint?

What is holiness?

'Holy' is among the most misunderstood words in the English language. We have holy socks, holy smoke, holy Joes, holy wars and holy cows. I even discovered an advertisement on the Internet advertising holy toast. The advertisement tells me that 'often it takes a suicidal leap of faith to see my chosen deity appear in my breakfast'. So why should I 'leave it to chance or random benevolence?' All I need to do is to leave it to 'an unblessed pair of Holy Toast presses'.

The site goes on to claim that these presses will guarantee a 'highly visible (even to the faithless) and perfect Virgin Mary' every time I want some toast. I simply 'press the bread into the mould, pop it into the toaster and, with no miracle whatsoever' my toast will become an icon. This, they say, 'is definitely the best thing that's happened to breakfast since sliced bread'. But a warning is added – I must not put the mould in the toaster or it will melt.

The word 'holy' is seriously misused in this advertisement. It encourages the false notion that holiness is a mystic quality conferred on people and, by association, on objects. The toast is considered holy because it now bears the image of the Virgin

Mary. It is true, of course, that inanimate objects may be considered holy. The vessels and robes used in the temple in Jerusalem, for example, were regarded as holy because of their use in the worship of God. But personal holiness has to do with the quality of the inner life and practical daily living. That is to say, it has to do with our relationship with God and others.

Personal holiness by association, like personal guilt by association, is a fallacy. If I befriend a criminal, it does not make me guilty of his crimes. Jesus, for example, could not be regarded as defiled just because he mixed with fraudulent tax-gatherers and prostitutes. In the same way, I do not become holy just because I befriend a holy person or approve of his lifestyle.

The only exception to this is the family. 'For the unbelieving husband has been sanctified through his wife, and the unbelieving wife has been sanctified through her believing husband. Otherwise your children would be unclean, but as it is, they are holy' (1 Cor. 7:14). However, the exception is easily misunderstood. Paul is simply making the point that the children of a Christian parent are not in the same category as the children of the godless. The word 'holy' in this context means 'hallowed'. No inner transformation is implied, as it would be if the word holy were used of the Christian parent.

Space does not permit a survey of the many errors that are circulating about holiness. But it is worth mentioning the false belief that if you want to be holy, you must be aloof! You must opt out of sinful society so that you are not tainted by it. But if holiness means withdrawal from society, Jesus himself could not be regarded as holy because he was the friend of sinners.

One day, some years ago, I was visiting from door to door. To avoid the need for explanation on the doorstep, I was wearing my clerical collar. At one house, a young woman came to the door in answer to my knock and invited me in. She was dressed in a very short skirt and had a very revealing neckline. Once inside, I was introduced to another woman who was dressed in the same way. She was feeding a baby. Was this a house of ill-repute, I wondered?

When I knocked at the house next door, the woman also invited me in. She was elderly and, as I soon discovered, she was a member of the local Methodist Church. I shall never forget her first words: 'Oh! Vicar,' she said, in a tone that reflected her deep concern, 'you haven't been in the house next door, have you?' She proceeded to confirm my suspicions about the house in some detail. She was clearly of the opinion that men in my position should stay away from such places!

When is a saint a saint?

Again, to understand the question we have to remember the different shades of meaning attaching to the word 'saint'. As soon as a person is born of the Spirit of God, he becomes a saint. This is because he now belongs to God and is set apart for him. He is accepted as a holy person because his sins have been washed away. God now sees him as being 'in Christ' which means that Christ's righteousness is credited to the sinner's account. It is like being covered from head to foot in a pure white robe from heaven that hides all our transgressions from view.

But God's purpose now is to make him into a saint in his character; to make him more like Jesus. When he repented and turned to Christ for forgiveness, he was anything but holy in his person. Now, he must move from being accepted by God as if he were holy, to being holy in his own life and conduct. This is a life-long process that now begins in earnest. Therefore, we may say that every person made a saint by the grace of God at conversion, is then called to become a saint in their ongoing life.

The question at the head of this chapter, therefore, has two answers. A saint is a saint as soon as he is accepted into God's family. But it is also true to say that a saint becomes a saint as he grows into the likeness of Christ. 'Personal holiness' makes the difference between a saint – an unworthy sinner whom God accepts as if he were righteous – and a saint – a believer who is growing into the likeness of Jesus. If the saint (in the first sense) does not become a saint (in the second sense), we have good reason to reject his claim to be a believer in the first place.

The example of Christ

The incarnation of Christ is the most amazing condescension the world has ever known or ever will know. He, 'being in very nature God, did not consider equality with God something to be grasped, but made himself nothing, taking the very nature of a servant, being made in human likeness' (Phil. 2:6-7). That God should become a servant for my sake is something I believe but cannot comprehend.

That he should lay aside his glory and suffer the cruellest form of execution known to man to rescue me from sin and death leaves me dumbfounded but deeply grateful. 'And being found in appearance as a man, he humbled himself and became obedient to death – even death on a cross!' (Phil. 2:8). What then can I say when I realise that he also became a curse for me? For 'Christ redeemed us from the curse of the law by becoming a curse for us, for it is written: "Cursed is everyone who is hung on a tree"' (Gal. 3:13).

These words of Paul focus our minds on the sacrificial love of God to such an extent that we tend to overlook the fact that Jesus is also the supreme example of personal holiness. His entire life on earth was a pattern for us to follow (1 Peter 2:21). The lessons we may learn from him are all relevant to our lives here and now, in the post-modern world.

It is a sad fact that many believers are not well informed about the earthly life of Christ. So much false information is circulating about his life these days, it is all too easy to accept it without checking it against the Gospel narratives. If we are to be imitators of Christ, the first thing to do is to start reading the Gospels so that we become familiar with the behaviour and teaching of Jesus.

Like Jesus, we must be humble and 'willing to associate with people of low position' (Rom. 12:16). Like him, we must set a pattern for others to follow as we live for God in the High Street. Like him, we must be heavily involved in the world, yet untainted by it. Like him, we must befriend sinners (Matt. 11:19), rejoicing with those who rejoice and mourning with those who mourn (Rom.12:15).

When Jesus was insulted, he did not retaliate; when he suffered, he made no threats (1 Peter 2:23). He was never bad-tempered, never complaining and never deceitful. Indeed, 'no deceit was found in his mouth' (1 Peter 2:22). Not least, his love for his people was, and still is, intense and everlasting. It certainly follows that 'since God so loved us, we also ought to love each other' (1 John 4:11).

2. Imitating Christ

What makes a saint a saint?

Personal holiness is being saintly in character

Did you hear about Shambo the holy cow? The poor beast contracted tuberculosis and had to be slaughtered. This decision by the authorities (in July 2007) raised very strong objections because the cow lived in a Hindu temple in Wales, and Hindus regard the cow as holy.

According to the *Oxford Dictionary of World Religions* (John Bowker, Oxford University Press, 2005), the cow is so regarded because it 'is revered as the source of food and symbol of life'. Accordingly, the Hindus are urging the government not to slaughter animals affected by foot and mouth disease, but to find alternative ways of dealing with the problem.

Now, if we use the word 'holy' to describe the character of people whom God has called to himself, in what way does this differ from the holiness of the cow? As we saw in the last chapter, in Christian terminology the word 'holy' has different shades of meaning. It may describe a person, an object or a place that is set apart for a sacred purpose. The first room in the Jewish temple, for example, was known as the Holy Place and 'Behind the second curtain was a room, called the Most Holy Place' (Heb 9:3). The word may also be used as a synonym for godliness.

Shambo was regarded as 'holy' by the Hindus because of his connection with their temple. But 'holy cow' cannot possibly mean 'saintly cow' or 'godly cow'. Cows are no more saintly than cats or dogs. Godliness or holiness is the outcome of a living relationship with God and although cows are God's creatures, they cannot know anything about this.

The apostle John says: 'We proclaim to you what we have seen and heard, so that you also may have fellowship with us. And our fellowship is with the Father and with his Son, Jesus Christ' (1 John 1:3). The purpose of proclaiming the gospel is fellowship with God and with one another. Those who repent and believe are brought into fellowship with God and with his church. It has been called vertical and horizontal fellowship.

Now, to have fellowship with God is to be holy. The enjoyment of this astonishing privilege is impossible for beasts. It is not even possible for those humans who are strangers to the grace of God. Therefore, it is ridiculous to talk about cows being called to holiness. Saints are called and enabled by God to be holy in everything they do, whereas cows can only do what cows do.

Saints imitate saints

We see then, that a saint is someone who is in fellowship with God and his children. Nothing and no one else can know anything about personal holiness. This being the case, younger saints have a double privilege. They not only have the example of Jesus, but of older saints as well – that is, those who are now (at least to some extent) saints in character as well as name.

This immediately raises the question of the importance of example. In recent times, it has been overlooked far too often. Many saints seem to have forgotten that they are constantly being watched, not only by the neighbours and the people they work with, but also by their own children. Our children take more notice of our habits and activities than we think. If we behave badly we should not be surprised if they follow our example.

Paul's conscience was clear about his standard of life. This is why he could confidently say, 'Follow my example, as I follow the example of Christ' (1 Cor. 11:1). This may come as a surprise to us. Even if we know we are good at something, we tend to think it is arrogant to say so. But Paul was not inhibited in this way. Having learned how to behave as a Christian by keeping his eyes on Jesus, he feels qualified to tell the Corinthians that they must learn by keeping their eyes on Paul! This is an essential characteristic of Christian leadership. The Revised Standard Version translates it like this: 'Be imitators of me, as I am of Christ.' I wonder if we are so confident that our example is worth following.

Some years ago, some friends of mine were going on holiday and asked if my wife and I would look after their parrot. After only two or three days' residence the bird had copied my wife calling my name, as she would do when I was in the study and a meal was ready. The imitation was so good that on occasions I had some difficulty in detecting whether it was my wife or the parrot calling me.

Learning by imitation is a recognised method for human beings too. As we would expect, it is frowned upon in some circles. The success of the method depends entirely on two things – first, the standard of the one who sets the example and, second, the faithfulness of the imitator in reproducing it. Evidently, Paul the apostle was convinced that we could learn by this method.

In another place, the apostle tells us to 'Be imitators of God' (Eph. 5:1). Of course, several aspects of God's holiness cannot be imitated. For example, God is unapproachable in his essence. He is 'the blessed and only Ruler, the King of Kings and Lord of Lords, who alone is immortal and who lives in unapproachable light, whom no-one has seen or can see' (1 Tim. 6:15-16). This is why people in the Old Testament feared for their lives when God came too near for comfort (Exod. 20:19). It is true that God revealed his glory to Moses, but only partially. We are told that God caused all his goodness to pass in front of Moses, but God told him: 'You cannot see my face, for no-one may see me and live' (Exod. 33:20).

We are given several examples in Scripture of the reaction of mere mortals when God drew near to them. Immediately, they became keenly aware of their impurity. When the prophet Isaiah had a vision of the Lord seated on a throne, he cried out, 'Woe to me! I am ruined! For I am a man of unclean lips, and I live among a people of unclean lips, and my eyes have seen the King, the LORD Almighty' (Isa. 6:5). But none of this means that we cannot learn from what the Scriptures reveal of the glory and character of God.

We shall see later that saints grow into the likeness of Christ by keeping him in sight. Beholding the glory of Christ is a proper use of the faith God has given us. It is also a proper use of the Scriptures. It is here, in God's Word, that Jesus is revealed to the eye of faith. This exercise makes us feel like Moses and Isaiah when they saw the Lord because now we too are seeing ourselves as we really are. That is to say, keeping Jesus in all his glory in constant view is a never-ending purifying process.

3. Sham saints

When is a saint not a saint?

When the White Queen in Lewis Carroll's *Through the Looking Glass*, told Alice that she was a hundred and one years, five months and a day old, Alice said she could not believe it. "'Can't you?" the Queen said in a pitying tone. "Try again: draw a long breath, and shut your eyes." Alice laughed. "There's no use trying", she said "one can't believe impossible things." "I daresay you haven't had much practice," said the Queen. "When I was your age, I always did it for half an hour a day. Why, sometimes I've believed as many as six impossible things before breakfast"'.

Now who was right, Alice or the queen? Surely, it is possible to believe that someone can live for a hundred and one years, five months and a day. But what if the queen had said she was two hundred and one years, five months and a day old? Would it have been possible to believe this? I guess most of us have met people who believe truly impossible things.

Jesus tells us that with God, all things are possible (Matt. 19:26). But what is possible with God is not always possible for us. And the (humanly) impossible things that God does always have purpose. We believe, for example, that Jesus walked on water in order to strengthen the faith of his disciples (Matt. 14:22-32). What we do not believe, however, is that God would do impossible things just for the sake of it – things that have no purpose.

Is it possible for a saint to be lost?

Christians have argued for centuries about whether Christians can fall from grace. Some insist that it is possible that those who have been born of the Holy Spirit into the family of God can lose their privileged status. Others, on good scriptural grounds, strenuously disagree. To be born and then to be unborn, or, to put it another way, to become a saint and then cease to be a saint, is an impossible thing.

Since it would serve no purpose, why would God do it? Why should he perform meaningless miracles? Why would he give new life and then take it away? Why would he start something good and not finish it (Phil. 1:6)? Why would he choose his children before the world began and then go back on his choice? We believe therefore, that such things are impossible even for God, for the simple reason that he cannot work against himself. Once a saint, always a saint!

Jesus said: 'My sheep listen to my voice; I know them, and they follow me. I give them eternal life, and they shall never perish; no-one can snatch them out of my hand' (John 10:27-28). I once quoted this text to a friend who believed it possible to fall away and be lost. She said, 'Ah! But you can snatch yourself out.' Now that really would be an impossible thing. Not only that, it is a deliberate manipulation of Jesus' words.

We do not deny of course, that some make a profession of faith that may last for a time – even a long time – and then fall away. They had claimed to be saints, and it is often difficult, if not impossible, to know whether their claims were genuine or not. But when this happens, either they are true believers who are backsliding, in which case they will be restored, or they were never truly born again in the first place.

Man-made saints

For those readers who have a Roman Catholic background, I should stress that we are talking about saints who are alive in this world right now. We have nothing to do with the Pope's claim to canonise people; that is to say, to make people into saints long after they are dead. According to the system, qualifications for their sainthood include the performance of miracles at their tombs, which are the result of the saints' prayers! These are also impossible things.

Many will remember that Christopher was venerated as a saint for very many years until, in 1969, his name was removed from the list because it could not be proved that he had ever existed, and even if he did, there is no evidence that he lived a holy life. But of course, since the Pope claims to be infallible, he cannot admit an error! To make such an admission would mean that he is not infallible after all. Therefore Christopher is still venerated as a saint even though his name is not on the list!

Those who believe in St Christopher, say that he was a tall and strong middle-aged man with a long beard, who spent his time carrying people across a river on his shoulders. On one occasion, a little child approached him and asked to be taken across. To Christopher's surprise, the child became heavier and heavier until the poor man found the weight unbearable. When he asked the child why he was so heavy, he told Christopher that it was because he had the weight of the world's sin on his shoulders! He was none other than the holy Christ child! Because of his noble service, Christopher was made the patron saint of travellers everywhere. 'Behold St Christopher and go on your way in safety' became the catchphrase of millions.

It is difficult not to feel sorry for those countless millions of travellers who still superstitiously regard Christopher as their patron saint. They are putting their trust in a legendary person to keep them safe all through life's journeys, and that is a tragedy. Such is the power of superstition, however, that many people *want* to go on trusting in a non-existent saint to keep them safe because they like it this way. Some refuse to believe that he never lived but others, it seems, are not particularly bothered whether he existed or not so long as the church says it is still safe to trust him.

Certainly, the production of St Christopher medals is still a profitable business. They can still be seen hanging in many car windows today. Meanwhile, the Roman Catholic Church is still canonising. Apparently, Pope John Paul made nearly three hundred saints during his papacy.

The trouble we have with all this is that the true and Biblical meaning of the word 'saint' is lost. It is God, not the Pope, who makes saints. And God does it while people are still living, not after they are dead. Once made, they are saints forever. Every true saint who lived, or still lives, on this earth is God's handiwork and his alone.

Think seriously about this: If you do not become a real saint in this life, you will certainly never become one in the next.

Bogus saints

I have a friend who admits to being naughty (her word) in earlier life and that she felt guilty about it. Now, however, the guilt feelings have gone because she thinks she has made up the loss by doing good. 'I think', she says, 'that the good now outweighs the bad, so I shall be OK'. Even so, she would not claim to be a saint – at least, not yet!

Millions in our world think in the same way. Sainthood is something acquired by our own efforts. The trouble is, no one seems to know they have acquired the status, and therefore the hope of 'being OK' cannot have any substance. For those who live on this false principle, living in uncertainty is inevitable.

No one would deny that there is a lot of 'good' in human nature. Aunt Bessie doesn't believe anything, but she is ever so generous and kind! The image of God in which we were created has not been entirely obliterated. Yet, although we use the word 'good' for the more attractive side of aunt Bessie's nature, what she does is never good enough for God. Even every 'good' act of hers is flawed by sin.

We call it 'good' because it contrasts with the extremes of human wickedness. But when Paul realised his inability to do good, he was thinking of the good that is acceptable to God: 'I know that nothing good lives in me, that is, in my sinful nature' (Rom. 7:18). He was admitting that, apart from the indwelling Spirit of God, he was incapable of getting anywhere near the standard God requires.

The same apostle tells us that 'when Gentiles, who do not have the law, do by nature things required by the law, they are a law for themselves' (Rom. 2:14). The commandments were not revealed to the godless Gentiles. Nevertheless, because they were created in the image of God, they had an inner sense of right and wrong; sometimes they approved of their own actions and at other times they strongly disapproved. In other words, they did not reach their own standard.

Paul's admission comes in the middle of his argument that both Jew and Gentile are guilty before God. The apostle is concerned to prove that both – those who have the commandments and those who do not – are in the same boat. The Gentiles have what we might call a natural standard but they do not reach it. The Jews have the divine standard and they do not reach it either. All are guilty of sin.

For this reason, it is impossible for the natural man, religious or otherwise, to grow in holiness. Any claim he makes to sainthood is bogus. A standard of morality attained by anyone in his own strength is not holiness. Nor can it act as a measure of holiness. Where there is no spiritual life, there can be no spiritual growth.

Some years ago, a friend of mine, an embalmer by trade, took me into his workplace. What goes on in these places is normally hidden from the public. Most people would probably not want to know anyway. He showed me the various tools of his trade and how he drained the blood from the corpse and replaced it with spirit. I also saw several open coffins containing examples of his work. All the bodies looked radiant in health. They looked as if a little nudge would wake them up. But they remained silent and motionless. So it is with those who are spiritually dead. No matter how good they may look, they are incapable of making a move toward God. Therefore, they cannot live holy lives.

We approve of the 'good' things that unbelievers do. Indeed, they should be encouraged. Our country would be a better place if the example set by many who are not Christians were followed. But since they are deeds done by people who are spiritually dead, they are not acceptable to God. This fact is unpalatable to many, but the Scriptures are unambiguous about it.

To put it another way, the only habits that are considered 'good' in the sight of God are the fruit of his Holy and life-giving Spirit. Other patterns of life – perhaps learned in a morally respectable family, a good school, or even as a result of religious influence – are not created by the Spirit. Without faith, it is impossible to please God (Heb. 11:6).

By contrast, believers soon discover that with God, all things are possible (Matt. 19:26). This obviously excludes things that are evil, like lying. He implants a permanent and supernatural principle of holiness in the hearts of all the members of his family that has nothing to do with our natural habits. He inclines the mind and will to live for God. This is the real difference between believer and unbeliever.

Now, since 'without holiness no-one will see the Lord' (Heb. 12:14), it follows that there is no hope for the unbeliever. Only those who live the new life of the Spirit qualify to enter God's presence. Their deeds are certainly not perfect. The handicap imposed on us by our sinful nature prevents us from attaining perfection. But in Christ there is full and free forgiveness for all our sins and this means that God accepts Christ's perfect obedience as if it were ours.

4. Clearing the fog

Do saints learn from the past?

Henry Ford (1863-1947) is not only well known as the founder of the Ford Motor Company, but also for his verdict on history. His exact words appeared in the Chicago Tribune in 1916: 'History is more or less bunk. It's tradition. We don't want tradition. We want to live in the present, and the only history that is worth a tinker's damn is the history that we make today.' Was he right?

A Spanish philosopher, born in the same year as Henry Ford, by the name of George Santayana (1863-1952), came to the opposite conclusion. In 1905 he wrote: 'Those who cannot remember the past are condemned to repeat it.' It is just another way of saying, 'those who do not learn from the mistakes of the past will make the same ones in the future.'

Of course, Ford was right to say that we want to live in the present. But to suggest that we cannot learn from the past is a serious error of judgment. This is certainly the case when it comes to understanding Christian holiness. In the past, several mistakes were made, and some of the errors were serious. If we are prepared to learn from them, we shall be better equipped to live in the present. We can learn a great deal from the teaching and the blunders of the saints of former years.

In this chapter, we try to clear up some of the misunderstandings.

A peep into the past

The theologians of the first five centuries of the Christian church, excluding the New Testament writers, are known as the Church fathers. It is called the Patristic Period. Oddly enough, they did not write very much on the subject of sanctification. But what they did write reveals an astonishing ignorance on some basic issues.

The most serious mistake was their failure to distinguish between faith and good deeds in the salvation of the sinner. 'What's wrong with that?' you ask. They were right in linking the two together because they belong together. They were wrong to confuse them when answering the question, 'how can sinners be saved?'

Follow me carefully. True faith always leads to good deeds, but the sinner is not saved by his good deeds. Nor is he saved by faith plus good deeds. Yet every saint needs to be clear about this, that if the person who claims to have faith in Christ does not begin to do good, we are right to conclude that his faith is not genuine. Genuine faith always leads to holy living, for 'without holiness no-one will see the Lord' (Heb. 12:14). Since some argue that this means we are saved by faith and good deeds, let us consider why such a statement leads to confusion.

What would we say, for example, about a person who puts his trust in Jesus Christ for salvation and is then killed in a road accident? He has not been given time to prove that his life has changed and that good deeds will follow. Is he saved? If his faith was genuine – and God alone would know – then the answer is an emphatic 'yes'. We maintain, therefore, that salvation is by faith alone (Eph. 2:8).

This was certainly true of the dying thief. He trusted in Christ in the hour of death. He turned to Jesus and said, 'Jesus, remember me when you come into your kingdom.' Jesus replied: 'I tell you the truth, today you will be with me in paradise' (Luke:23:43).

The Bible is clear however, that justification (being put right with God) by faith in Christ is followed by sanctification (being set apart for God and beginning to live a holy life.) The thoughtful reader will now see that to say a person is saved by both faith and deeds confuses justification with sanctification.

When a person is justified by faith, his sins, past present and future, are forgiven and that is the end of the matter. No one will be able to bring a charge against him, not even if he drops dead the day after he is justified. Listen to the apostle's triumphant words: 'Who will bring any charge against those whom God has chosen? It is God who justifies. Who is he that condemns?' Or, as the Good News Bible puts it: 'Who then, will condemn them?' (Rom. 8:33-34).

Someone may ask: 'If faith always leads to holy living, why does the saint need continuing forgiveness? Surely, if he is a holy person, he will not sin. The answer is simple. No matter how holy a person becomes he will never be free from sin in this life. This may create a problem for those who are not believers, but that is because their understanding of sin is limited. They do not grasp that sin is failing to maintain God's high standard.

And what is this standard? It is to love God 'with all your heart, and with all your soul and with all your mind' and to love 'your neighbour as yourself' (Matt. 22:37-39). Obviously, to achieve this standard, I would need to comply with the commandments every minute of my life. I cannot claim to have reached it for a single moment. Sinless perfection is unattainable in this life. No matter how holy he becomes, the saint will need God's forgiveness every day of his life.

One error leads to another

The mistake made by the early fathers is natural. We sinners are prone to think of ourselves as being more capable than we really are. Oh yes, we say, we can live good lives anytime we choose! We can contribute a lot to our salvation! The fact is that, by nature, we are completely helpless in this matter. And the sooner we identify with the apostle Paul, who admitted that nothing good lived in his old sinful nature, the better it will be for us (Rom. 7:18).

Paul is here speaking as a new man in Christ. He is saying that all the good in his life as a Christian is due entirely to the grace of God. Believers who, in their ignorance, take credit for the good in their lives, are guilty of slighting the work of the Holy Spirit.

The death of Christ then, is not only the basis on which God justifies the believing sinner; it is also the source of his sanctification. 'For we know' says Paul, 'that our old self was crucified with him (Christ) so that the body of sin might be done away with, that we should no longer be slaves to sin...' (Rom. 6:6).

Here the apostle is saying that the old sinful nature is dead. That proud old 'I' must be crucified if we are to make progress in holiness. All the saints are in such vital union with Christ, that his death is their death. The old life is dead and buried. It ceased to exist when we were born again. The same is true of Christ's resurrection. In the previous verse, the apostle says: 'If we have been united with him like this in his death, we will certainly be united with him in his resurrection' (Rom. 6:5). Paul also teaches that the old nature is still alive. We shall look at the apparent contradiction later.

Take both verses together and we see that sharing in Christ's death and resurrection is not merely a wonderful doctrine, but also a thrilling experience. We simply cannot share in the benefits of his death without also sharing in the blessings of his resurrection. It is impossible to die with Christ and not to live with him here and now.

The failure of the early fathers to understand this led to further errors, some of them destructive. For example, asceticism – the attempt to become holy by separating yourself from society and living a life of rigorous austerity – thrived on the idea that holiness could be achieved by self-effort. There is nothing wrong, of course, with self-denial, but the idea of permanently denying to oneself the normal and harmless pleasures of life in the belief that we may be able to love God more perfectly, shows a deplorable ignorance of Scripture.

The notion of ministers in the church being sacrificing priests, as they were in the Old Testament, also arose in this period, and for the same reason. For if the sanctification of the saints is not directly related to the death and resurrection of Christ, the doors are wide open to all sorts of priestcraft. Sadly, these destructive errors are still with us.

The Reformation

Apart from some helpful developments in the writings of men like Augustine (354-430) and Thomas Aquinas (1225-74), a clear distinction between faith and good deeds – between justification and sanctification – was not made until the Reformation. The reformers rightly saw justification as an act of God, affecting the legal status of every believer, and sanctification as a moral transformation in the believer's life in the power of the Holy Spirit. They also recognised the direct link between the two.

Martin Luther (1483-1546)

These precious truths finally illuminated the darkened mind of a monk named Martin Luther. He had left no stone unturned in order to find peace with God, but it eluded him. Praying, fasting, confessing his sins and punishing his body led him nowhere. Finally, he lighted on Paul's words in Romans chapter one: 'For in the gospel a righteousness from God is revealed, a righteousness that is by faith from first to last, just as it is written, "The righteous will live by faith"' (verse 17). At long last, Luther understood that God accepted him, just as he was, by faith alone.

As we would expect, the great reformer also understood that the faith that justifies is never alone because sanctification inevitably follows. But he never again confused justification and sanctification because he now knew that even the good deeds that followed after justification contributed nothing to it. They were the evidence that his faith was genuine.

John Calvin (1509-64)

'What is your theological persuasion?' I put this question to a man who was interested in joining the staff of the church where I served. Instead of answering my question, he proceeded, with some disdain, to tell me what it wasn't! 'I am not a Calvinist' he began. Evidently, he thought Calvinists were such a bad lot I would be more than pleased to agree with him. It was a foolish assumption!

The attitude is common. Many think that the only lesson we can learn from Calvin is a negative one – don't get involved with the subject of election! The great reformer is dismissed without being given a hearing. No doubt Calvin, like all good men, made some errors of judgment, but his teaching on justification and sanctification is as sound as a bell. Indeed, from his pen we have a thoroughly Biblical statement of both doctrines and of the vital link between the two.

Let the man speak for himself: 'When Paul declares that we were chosen in Christ before the foundation of the world (Eph. 1:4), he certainly shows that no regard is had to our own worth; since in the whole seed of Adam our heavenly Father found nothing worthy of his election, he turned his eye on his own Anointed, that he might select as members of his body those whom he was to assume into the fellowship of life ... Since election precedes that divine grace by which we are made fit to obtain immortal life, what can God find in us to induce him to elect us? ... God, says he, "hath chosen us in him before the foundation of the world that we might be holy and without blame before him in love…"' (Eph. 1:4-5). (*Institutes of the Christian Religion*, Eerdmans Publishing Co., 1975 Vol. 2, Book III, pp. 213-4.)

I challenge anyone to find fault with this biblically. It is obvious to any fair-minded reader that Calvin added nothing to Paul's words. So if Calvin is extreme, then so is the apostle. I submit, therefore, that the lessons we learn from Calvin have to do with our being faithful to the entire Scripture to the best of our ability.

John Wesley (1703-91)

Along with his friend and fellow preacher, George Whitefield (1714-70), John Wesley achieved great things for God in both Europe and the United States. Like Luther before him, he came to see that justification is by faith alone. After being an Anglican minister for about ten years, he met Peter Bohler, a Moravian minister, whose influence led to Wesley's conversion in 1738.

I mention John Wesley in this brief peep into history because, although he was a man greatly used by God, his views on sanctification were decidedly odd. He seems to have believed in instantaneous and entire sanctification, which means that a believer may become a perfect saint in name and character in a moment. He assumed that since justification is a complete work of God in response to faith, sanctification must follow the same pattern and on this basis, he regarded it as a second work of grace.

A difficulty arises because Wesley also regarded sanctification as progressive. To my mind, an answer to the contradiction is not possible. It is only fair to point out, however, that Wesley's idea of entire sanctification related to our love for God and others and not to our inner thoughts. Even so, it is hard to conceive of perfect love being sustained all through life, even on that basis.

From his teaching on this subject, the idea of holiness as a 'second blessing' spread widely. Many people, including me, were deceived by it. It promised more than it could deliver because no saint on earth, if he were honest, would be able to claim perfect love. The Christian is better equipped to identify sin than anyone. And, in the nature of the case, the more we love God and others, the more conscious we become of our own shortfall.

It is also difficult to understand how such a separation between our love for God and others on the one hand, and our inner thoughts on the other would work. Since our thoughts are usually the spring of our actions, such a separation is unnatural. For example, if I entertain, even for a moment, an evil thought about someone, how could I claim to love him perfectly?

5. Born of God

Where do saints come from?

I have a vivid memory of driving up a hill in Derbyshire. The road was unfenced. A wide expanse of grazing land stretched away into the distance on both sides of the road. Just ahead, near a bend in the road, a rocky outcrop protruded through the grass. Why should I remember this place in such detail? There was nothing special about it. It was a pleasant scene, but no more beautiful than the scenery we had been passing for some miles.

The reason is that just as I was approaching the bend in the road, my daughter, who was sitting in the back seat with her younger sister, said: 'Dad, where do babies come from?' Trying not to sound hesitant, and not being inclined to take refuge in the stork legend, I adopted the policy of giving her just enough information to satisfy her curiosity. 'They come out of mummy's tummy', I replied. This, however, did not satisfy her. 'But how do they get there?' she persisted. Is there any wonder I remember the place?

Situations like this have kept the stork legend alive. Certainly, in the past when young children wanted to know where babies came from, many parents, not knowing what to say, fobbed them off with the fairy tale. The poor youngsters whose parents still take refuge in such tales, believe all sorts of weird stories about the origin of babies.

The saints' true origin

'Where do saints come from?' The question may not be quite as embarrassing but it is, nevertheless, a question most people would not know how to answer. Indeed, the very word 'saint', like the word 'holy', is another of the most misunderstood words in the English language. Some of the answers given are no less fantastic than the stork legends.

We have considered the false claim made by the Roman Catholic Church, that only the Pope is able to make saints. Other religions too have their own ideas. Hindus believe that human beings attain sainthood by their own efforts. Ramakrishna (1836-86), for example, is regarded as a man who achieved his sainthood by exploring many different methods of approaching God. Hindus see him as an outstanding saint.

People who are not influenced by the teaching of the various religions, – and that is probably the majority in our western civilisation – think of a saint as a person who is exceptionally patient and kind, especially when under trial. Usually, when we hear people say 'so and so is a saint', the comment has little to do with religion. It is just a matter of a person's consistent goodness being noticed and appreciated.

We said in the last chapter that a person becomes a saint when he is born again of the Spirit of God. 'Born again', some will say, 'isn't this the language of eccentrics and extremists?' It is certainly true that the two words have been abused in our time, but we must not allow the abusers to call the tune. After all, they are the words of Jesus himself when he was in conversation with a deeply religious Pharisee called Nicodemus: 'I tell you the truth,' Jesus said to him, 'no-one can see the kingdom of God unless he is born again' (John 3:3).

One thing is certain – Jesus was not talking about physical rebirth. Nicodemus himself made this mistake. 'How can a man be born when he is old?' he asked. 'Surely he cannot enter a second time into his mother's womb to be born!' (John 3:4). Jesus went on to explain that he was talking about the new life from God that the Holy Spirit gives. The new birth is the miracle God performs in the life of every one who repents and believes the gospel. It has nothing to do with being born into a human family but everything to do with being born into God's family.

Natural birth is something that happened to all of us. Yet, even though someone is being born every few seconds, we are still amazed at the birth of a child. Although we may understand the process of development in the womb, there is still a mystery about it. The new birth, however, only happens to some of us, and it is even more amazing and mysterious. Like natural birth, it is God's handiwork, but unlike natural birth, it is totally beyond our comprehension.

Jesus compared it to the wind. He said to Nicodemus: 'The wind blows wherever it pleases. You hear its sound, but you cannot tell where it comes from or where it is going. So it is with everyone born of the Spirit' (John 3:8). Just as we have no control over the wind, so we have no control over the Spirit. We feel the wind and see it blowing things around, but we cannot see the wind itself. In a similar way, we feel the effect of the Spirit's work in the new birth and see the difference he makes, but we cannot see the Spirit. The process remains a mystery to us.

But there's more. The apostle Peter tells the Christians to whom he writes: 'For you have been born again, not of perishable seed, but of imperishable, through the living and enduring word of God' (1 Peter 1:23). This means that the Holy Spirit gives new life through God's living Word, the Bible. There is no contradiction here. People are indeed born again by trusting in Jesus Christ but the Christ in whom we trust is the Christ we read about in the Bible. There is no other Christ. God's Holy Spirit and God's holy Word work together in producing and sustaining the new life.

God's Spirit and God's Word cannot be separated. Those who claim to be led by the Spirit but do not open the Bible are deceiving themselves. It is possible, of course, to have the Spirit without having access to the written Word. This is the unhappy situation of believers in countries where the Bible is banned. But even in these circumstances, the believer is aware of the role of Scripture in his life and longs for the day when he can possess a Bible of his own.

It is not possible, however, to understand the Word without the Spirit. People who have some knowledge of the Scriptures, but are not born of the Spirit, are still in the dark. There may be some literary appreciation of certain older versions, but unspiritual people cannot understand spiritual principles. As Paul says, 'For the message of the cross is foolishness to those who are perishing' 1 Cor. 1:18). They have no light to illuminate the page.

The enlightenment of John Charles Ryle

John Charles Ryle (1816-1900), the first bishop of Liverpool, whose influence for the gospel is incalculable, is an excellent example of the power of the Word and the Spirit in the new birth. He became a saint as he was sitting in church feeling a bit down after an illness. The Scripture lesson was taken from the second chapter of Paul's letter to the Ephesians. When the reader came to verses eight and nine: 'For it is by grace you have been saved, through faith – and this not from yourselves, it is the gift of God – not by works, so that no-one can boast', Ryle's heart was opened.

Marcus Loane describes it like this: 'Ryle must have heard those words often enough before, but their point had been dulled by the confused murmur of the world all around. It was in the simple hearing of those words of Scripture that he grasped the secret of the Gospel, and that sudden discovery of the meaning of the grace of God was to make him a new man in a new world.' (*John Charles Ryle*, Hodder and Stoughton, 1983, p. 32).

A saint then is a person whose mind and heart have been enlightened by the Word and the Spirit. This does not mean that he understands everything in the Scriptures. Nor does it mean that he has suddenly become holy in his own right. No! He is still ignorant of many things and in the early stages his life is anything but holy.

Saints are sinners!

So someone may ask: 'If he is still a sinner, how can he be a saint?' As we saw in chapter 1, the saint is holy in the sense that he is now set apart to live for the glory of God. He becomes holy in this sense at the very moment he is born again. But just as a baby grows up to maturity, so everyone who is born again is called to grow up into a mature and holy person. Day by day, he is becoming more like Jesus.

In the first verse of Paul's letter to the Ephesians he says: 'Paul, an apostle of Christ Jesus by the will of God. To the saints in Ephesus…' (Eph. 1:1). Obviously, the apostle is not writing to a group of extra holy people in the church and ignoring the rest – a kind of church within a church. No, he is talking about all the born again sinners who make up the church in Ephesus. Every member is a saint.

Another example is found in 2 Corinthians 1:1. Paul is greeting the Corinthian Christians: 'Paul, an apostle of Christ Jesus by the will of God, and Timothy our brother, to the church of God in Corinth, together with all the saints throughout Achaia…'. Any reading of the Corinthian letters will show that the Christians in Corinth were far from perfect. Paul uses the word 'saints' without making any distinction on the basis that some may have been holier than others. They were all set apart for God.

We conclude then, that everyone in the world is in one of two groups. He is either a saint or an unbeliever. (By 'unbeliever' I mean a person who is not trusting in Christ alone for salvation.) Just as a person cannot be half born, so he cannot be half born again. If he is in the family of God, he is spiritually alive and therefore a saint. If he is not in the family, he is spiritually dead and is not a saint.

How then do we become saintly in our character? The apostle Peter stresses the role of Scripture: 'Like newborn babes, crave pure spiritual milk, so that, by it you may grow up in your salvation, now that you have tasted that the Lord is good (1 Peter 2:2-3). Peter is still thinking of the Word of God which, to born again believers is like wholesome milk to the newborn. We grow up into Christ by feeding regularly on his precious Word, the Bible.

The answer to the question, 'Where do saints come from?' should not now be in doubt. They are born from above! It is interesting to notice that the word 'again' in the phrase 'born again' (John 3:3 and 3:7), translates the Greek word *an'othen* which means 'above'. 'Born from above' would be a legitimate translation.

Only saints are sanctified

Having established where saints come from, it is not difficult to answer the question, 'Where are they going?' to which we shall come in Part Four. Is it not obvious that if they are born of God, they are also born for God? Heaven is their destiny. I mention this here so that the reader will be in no doubt that only saints are sanctified. Only those who are born of God are being prepared for the glory to come.

No matter how religious a person may be, unless he is a sincere believer in Jesus Christ as Saviour and Lord, he cannot know anything about true holiness. The elect – those whom God has given to his beloved Son – and no one else but the elect, are to be made holy. We should never confuse Christian holiness with moral 'goodness'.

Of course, today's saints are included in the elect. Jesus himself said so: 'My prayer is not for them [the apostles] alone. I pray also for those who will believe in me through their message, that all of them may be one...' (John 17:20-21). As we have seen, the Lord also prayed that all who belong to Christ would be sanctified by the truth, which is the Word of God (John 17:17).

One final thought before we move on. Readers who are concerned about their status before God and want to know the way of salvation, should never entertain the idea that they may not belong to God's elect. The new life is offered to all who will repent and believe the Gospel. And the very fact that you want to know more is, in itself, an indication that the Spirit is already at work in your life. No one can know that he has not been chosen before he turns to Christ. God's command to him is to repent and believe the gospel.

You may rely on the promise of Christ himself that whoever comes to him he will never drive away (John 6:37). If you believe in God, you must also believe 'that he rewards those who earnestly seek him' (Heb. 11:6). You may feel, rightly, that you do not deserve anything and have no strength to help yourself. But you can plead for mercy on the basis that God has promised to be merciful to repenting sinners. There is no other way to become a saint.

6. Sanctimonious or sanctified?

Are saints odd?

Sanctimonious old icebergs

Samuel Langhorne Clemens, otherwise known as Mark Twain (1839-1910), is a well-known American writer. The following is taken from his account of a forthcoming excursion to the Holy Land:

'Another passenger – a solemn, unsmiling, sanctimonious old iceberg that looked like he was waiting for a vacancy in the Trinity, as Henry Clapp said of Rev. Dr. Osgood – walked in the other day and stood around for some time, and finally said he had forgotten, when he took passage, to inquire if the excursion would come to a halt on Sundays. Captain Duncan replied that he hardly expected to anchor the ship in the middle of the Atlantic, but that on shore everybody would be free – no restrictions – free to travel on Sunday or not, just as they saw fit; and he had no doubt that some would do one and some the other.'

As it turned out, the passenger had no heartfelt desire to keep the Sabbath. He just wanted to avoid divine vengeance for travelling on the Lord's Day. Mark Twain comments: 'Now I respected that man's repugnance to violating the Sabbath until he betrayed that he would violate it in a minute if he were not afraid the lightning would strike him, or something else would happen to him, and then I lost my reverence for him.' (Mark Twain's correspondence with the San Francisco ALTA CALIFORNIA. Letter 26.)

Sanctity and sanctimony

What do you think – was this man sanctified or sanctimonious or both? Evidently, his religion was skin-deep. He had no desire to honour God by keeping the Sabbath day holy. He was miserable because he was afraid of the consequences of failing to do so. Mark Twain may have been right to call him 'sanctimonious', but 'sanctified' he certainly was not.

The sad thing is that many people confuse the two words. This is probably because several words come from the same root. We have sanctification, sanctity, sanctimony, sanctuary and the verbs and adjectives that are related to these nouns. To make matters worse, 'sanctimony' used to mean 'holiness' but the word has changed its meaning. Indeed, it is now used to describe a person who is trying to imitate a holy person, like the 'sanctimonious old iceberg' Mark Twain talks about.

The first thing to say about a sanctified person is this: He is a Spirit-filled person. God's Spirit lives in him. Since God is the author of his sanctification, he is also a kind and joyful person because 'the fruit of the Spirit is love, joy, peace, patience, kindness, goodness, faithfulness, gentleness and self-control' (Gal. 5:22). Unlike Mark Twain's sanctimonious old iceberg, a saint is also a person who takes God's commandments seriously.

Inevitably, attempts at 'do-it-yourself' sanctification are bound to produce a bogus kind of holiness. But it would be easier for pigs to fly than for sinners to re-create themselves in the image of God.

Like Mark Twain, people usually frown on sanctimonious old icebergs. Oddly enough, they often frown on people who are truly holy as well. When the word 'holiness' is mentioned, many people think instinctively of people who are narrow-minded killjoys. Even many people who are religious – using the word in its popular sense – regard holiness as taking things too far!

Jesus said: 'Whoever believes in me, as the Scripture has said, streams of living water will flow from within him. By this he meant the Spirit, whom those who believed on him were later to receive' (John 7:38-39). The believer will be warm-hearted and his life will overflow in blessings to those around him. Does this sound like a sanctimonious old iceberg?

Authentic imps?

You would probably be deeply hurt if I referred to your child as a little imp. The word 'imp' is now used to describe 'a mischievous child'. What then would you think of Thomas Cromwell who, in a letter to King Henry VIII, referred to the king's son as 'that noble imp'? Even worse, in an ancient prayer for the Prince of Wales, his royal highness is called 'that most angelic imp'. At first sight it might appear that the phrase was intended to mean 'naughty but nice' – just as we might say, 'he is a lovable rogue'.

All becomes clear when we realise that, originally, the word 'imp' meant 'a new shoot' and therefore a child. Obviously, since the meaning of the word now has mischief attached to it, we would refrain from using it to refer to someone else's child. But if that were not the case, we could legitimately refer to new saints as 'holy imps' – new shoots set apart for God.

Now when I say 'new' I do not mean re-cycled. A new shoot is a completely new beginning. As Paul says, '… if anyone is in Christ, he is a new creation; the old has gone, the new has come!' (2 Cor. 5:17). We do not become saints by patching up the old sinful nature and churning out the same old sins in a different order. On the contrary, we participate in God's nature (2 Peter 1:4). This does not mean that we have now become gods. It does mean that we have received the Spirit of Christ. We are newly born children.

Every saint is called to saintliness

The word 'saint' in the Greek language, from which our English New Testament is translated, is *hagios*. As we have seen, it refers to a person who is set apart for the service of God, and also to one who, having been set apart, is becoming holy in his character. Other English words may be used to translate *hagios*, as we shall see in a moment.

Indeed, the word 'saint' as it is used in the New Testament is inclusive. It describes all those who belong to Christ. Careful reading, however, will show that every saint is set to become saintly in character because God predestined him 'to be conformed to the likeness of his Son' (Rom. 8:29). That is what holiness is all about.

We may say, therefore, that every saint is called to saintliness (1 Thess. 4:7) There are no exceptions. It is a serious mistake to think that the call to holy living is just for a select few. Indeed, a saint's growth in personal godliness is the only external proof that he is a saint. With the exception of people like the dying thief who die immediately after they are born again, people who never become saintly are not saints and never have been. The writer to the Hebrews is uncompromising: 'Make every effort to live in peace with all men and to be holy; without holiness no-one will see the Lord' (Heb. 12:14).

Some more recent versions of the New Testament translate *hagios* with the two words 'holy ones'. This is almost certainly because of the erroneous meanings now attaching to the word 'saint'. For example, the old Authorised Version of 1 Thessalonians 3:13 speaks of our Lord Jesus Christ coming 'with all his saints' but the New International Version tells us that he is coming with 'all his holy ones'. It makes little difference. Both have the same meaning.

Invited or chosen?

Before we move on, it is important that we understand the difference between being invited and being chosen. The Greek verb translated invited is *kletos*, pronounced 'klay-tos', which really means 'called'. In Matthew chapter 22, Jesus tells the parable of the wedding banquet. The kingdom of heaven, he says, is like a king who prepared a wedding banquet for his son. When those who had been invited were told to come, they refused. The king was angry and sent his servants out to invite anyone they found. When the king came into the banqueting hall, he saw a man who was not wearing wedding clothes and gave instructions for him to be thrown out. The comment Jesus made is very revealing: 'For many are invited, but few are chosen' (Matt. 22:14). The chosen are the elect.

Care is needed here because the word 'called' may be translated by 'invited' or 'chosen'. For example, Paul says that 'those he predestined, he also called; those he called, he also justified; those he justified, he also glorified' (Rom. 8:30). Here, those who are 'called' are the elect or the chosen. Yet, the Authorised Version of Matt. 22:14 reads: 'For many are called, but few are chosen.' Here the 'called' are not the elect. The New International Version has updated this to 'For many are invited, but few chosen.'

True saints, therefore, are chosen by God and called (chosen) to live a holy life. They are always genuine in their response. But those who reject the invitation are not excused. On the contrary, God will hold them responsible for spurning his gracious invitation.

True humanity

I never cease to be amazed that so many intelligent people are prepared to believe that human beings are nothing more than well-developed apes. As long as this ridiculous notion is accepted as an established fact in our minds, we will never know what it means to be truly human.

Compassion, many believe, is the highest expression of humanness. On this basis, since Jesus Christ is the highest expression of compassion, to be like him is to be truly human. This is consistent with the teaching of Jesus: 'Greater love has no-one than this, that he lay down his life for his friends. You are my friends if you do what I command' (John 15:13-14). 'A new command I give you: Love one another. As I have loved you, so you must love one another' (John 13:34). Here Jesus sets the standard for his followers, not only in word but also in deed. Every saint knows, or should know, that this is what sanctification is all about.

This presents a serious problem for unbelievers, especially those who are advocates of the theory of evolution. They cannot explain the supposed transition from animal instinct to human consciousness. They are totally out of their depth when it comes to explaining the transition from the mind that is set on the desires of the sinful nature to the mind controlled by the Spirit (Rom. 8:5-7).

Only believers are aware of these things. They alone know what it means to 'participate in the divine nature and escape the corruption in the world caused by evil desires' (2 Peter 1:4). By contrast, those who believe we are nothing more than developed animals are more likely to behave like animals – the survival of the fittest and all that.

Jesus is the perfect human being. Therefore, it follows that saints are becoming more human by the day. Through the indwelling power of the Holy Spirit, our fallen humanity is being restored.

The more Christ-like we are, the more our true humanness will be seen. The less Christ-like we are, the more our sinful nature will be seen because sin is the destroyer of our humanity.

We conclude then that a saint is a human being. He is not an oddity, not peculiar (in the modern sense of the word) and certainly not a sanctimonious old iceberg. He begins as an authentic imp and grows into authentic saintliness.

7. Second-class saints?

Do all saints achieve the same level?

Equal calling?

The MCC (Marylebone Cricket Club), founded in 1787, is the oldest cricket club in the world. For over two centuries, women were excluded from membership. Several attempts were made to change the rules but without success – until September 1998. For various reasons, previous votes had not reached the two-thirds majority required. Now, at last, this has been achieved and women are no longer to be regarded as second-class, even if they are not as good at playing cricket as men!

Although there are deep differences of opinion about the role of women in the church, there is no argument about their admission to membership. When Paul said: 'There is neither Jew nor Greek, slave nor free, male nor female, for you are all one in Christ Jesus' (Gal. 3:28), he did not mean, as some argue, that these distinctions are abolished. This would not make sense. The apostle was insisting that whatever the nationality, rank or sex of believers, none has preference with God.

Therefore, the call to holiness comes to every believer. God does not predestine a select number of his saints to be recreated in the image of Christ. The call to holiness comes to all alike. It is true that holiness in men and women will express itself differently.

The masculinity of men will be refined, as will the femininity of women. The fact that they have different gifts does not alter the fact that both sexes are called to be holy. The notion that God calls some to be more holy than others is thoroughly unbiblical and must be rejected.

Equal privileges?

Are we right then to work on the principle that God expects more of some than he does of others? To answer in the affirmative we need only to take a look at the inequality of privilege in the worldwide church. It is a sad but observable fact. It means that some saints have greater access to the means of grace than others.

We are also mindful of the word of Jesus: 'From everyone who has been given much, much will be demanded; and from the one who has been entrusted with much, much more will be asked' (Luke 12:48). God *does* expect more from those who have the greater privileges.

It cannot be denied that some excel in holiness and others are left behind in the slough of mediocrity. In spite of the inequality of privilege however, it is not always those with an advantage that make the better progress. Another factor must be taken into account. There is a difference in their aspiration – in the strength of their desire to be like Jesus – which is not explained by their different gifts. Indeed, it is sometimes the gifted people who are left behind.

Pastor and people

We must carefully distinguish between the calling to holiness and the calling to specific tasks. Obviously, the pastor or teacher must be gifted for his task. As the apostle says, '… to each one of us grace has been given as Christ apportioned it... It was he who gave some to be apostles, some to be prophets, some to be evangelists, and some to be pastors and teachers...' (Eph. 4:7,11).

Naturally, pastors are expected to set the example in holy living. An ungodly pastor is a contradiction in terms. 'Since an overseer is entrusted with God's work, he must be blameless – not overbearing, not quick-tempered, not given to drunkenness, not violent, not pursuing dishonest gain. Rather, he must be hospitable, one who loves what is good, who is self-controlled, upright, holy and disciplined' (Titus 1:7-8).

But the apostle is certainly not saying that these qualities are not required in anyone else. It is just that when a pastor fails to maintain a high standard, he brings more scandal on the church than would be the case if someone with a less public profile is guilty of it. The standard of holiness to which we are called does not vary according to the task we are assigned.

Moreover, every saint, whatever his gifts, must commend the gospel. The effective witness of the church in the world, especially the local church, does not depend solely on its leadership. The testimony of the church is seriously weakened when the rank and file members indulge in petty squabbling, destructive criticism and behaviour of doubtful morality.

It is very interesting to notice what the apostles did when they were confronted with a disagreement in the church over the daily distribution of food to widows. They realised that to deal with it themselves would mean neglecting the ministry of the Word to which they were called. So they asked the church to choose seven men from the church with qualifications to accept this responsibility.

What were these qualifications? In stark contrast with the practice in so many churches today, there was no appeal for volunteers. The apostles did not ask any Tom, Dick or Harry who might be willing. The men chosen for the task had to be known as men 'full of the Spirit and wisdom' (Acts 6:3). There were not two different standards – one for preachers and another for serving tables.

We must go still further – the sanctification of each believer is vital to the healthy spiritual fellowship of those who truly love the Lord. That is to say, we all owe a duty of holy living to our brothers and sisters in Christ as well as to the Lord himself. It is his church and we are contributors to her well-being.

So 'let us consider how we may spur one another on towards love and good deeds. Let us not give up meeting together, as some are in the habit of doing, but let us encourage one another – and all the more as you see the Day approaching' (Heb. 10:24-25).

Part Two

God's plan for his saints

8. God's standard

The saints' aim

What is holiness?

In his well-known book on holiness, Bishop John Charles Ryle (1816-1900), the first bishop of Liverpool, defines its nature. It is the habit of being of one mind with God as he is revealed in the Scriptures. It is hating what God hates and loving what God loves. A holy person will strive to shun every known sin and to keep every known commandment. He will aim to be like our Lord Jesus Christ, which means he will be forgiving, unselfish, and will seek to do his Father's will.

The bishop goes on to point out that a holy person will be patient, gentle, kind, and in control of his tongue. He will be self-controlled, self-denying and work hard to control his passions and sinful inclinations. He will not stand on his rights, but will aim to behave towards others as he would like them to behave towards him. He will detest lying, slandering, infighting, cheating, dishonesty, and unfair dealing, even in little things.

The saintly person will be merciful and benevolent. He will always want to be useful and do what he can to meet the needs of others. He will never be idle. Purity of heart will be his desire. For this reason, he will turn away from filthiness and steer clear of temptation whenever it is in his power to do so. He will fear

God, not because he is afraid of God, but because he reveres and loves him. In humility, he will always be conscious of the evil in his heart and keenly aware that he does not deserve any of God's mercies and blessings.

Finally, he will be faithful in his duty and relationships because he knows he is the Lord's servant. Consequently, he will be a good husband and parent. Although he will not neglect his daily responsibilities, he will live as someone who has treasure in heaven. Not least, he will be a man of prayer and the Word (the Bible) and will love the fellowship of like-minded people. (*Holiness* by J. C. Ryle. Evangelical Press, Darlington, UK, 1979.)

Motivation

We need to add a brief word about the motive for holiness. Why should anyone want to be holy? The Scriptures are very clear that the saint obeys God's commands for one reason only – he loves God and has a strong desire that Christ should be honoured in his life. In other words, his longing to glorify Christ is his primary motivation.

The strength of motivation will vary among the saints because their understanding of what Christ has done for them also varies. The motivation of those who realise that we owe everything to God will be the stronger. Most believers would agree that the greatest expression of his love for us is the gift of his beloved Son to pay the price for our sins. But how much deeper is our gratitude once we understand that Christ died for us because God loved us before the world began and he did so in order to make us holy. 'For he chose us in him before the creation of the world to be holy and blameless in his sight' (Eph. 1:4).

As Paul explains, 'It is because of him [God] that you are in Christ Jesus, who has become for us wisdom from God – that is, our righteousness, holiness and redemption' (1 Cor. 1:30). Were it not for God's choice we would not be 'in Christ Jesus' in the first place. But now, being in Christ means that we become partakers of his wisdom, which, according to the apostle, has three excellent benefits. First, he is our righteousness because by his death the demands of divine justice are satisfied on our behalf. Second, he is our sanctification because the presence of his Spirit with us guarantees that we shall grow into his likeness. Third, he is our redemption, our final deliverance from everything that defiles.

Not only so, but we are also the beneficiaries of his intercession. Our cleansing was purchased for us by his death and everything we become in the way of holiness is due solely to his intercession. His prayer in John 17:17 will certainly prevail: 'Sanctify them by the truth; your word is truth.' Without this, we would get nowhere.

True holiness, therefore, is a result of what Christ has done for us and is motivated by loving gratitude. Any other motive for maintaining a standard of integrity and honesty cannot produce real holiness and the saint is soon in a position to distinguish true holiness from its counterfeits. Where there is no love for Christ, there can be no holiness. For example, if a person maintains high moral standards because his family have a reputation in society, his efforts may be commendable, but he cannot be called holy.

On a personal note, in recent years, the assurance that I am God's chosen one with all the above benefits and more, has brought such overwhelming joy to my heart that there is now nothing to compare with it. This experience does two things for me. First, it brings a feeling of regret that I did not previously make better progress. Second, it boosts my motivation so that I pray for grace to do better in whatever time is left for me.

The Ten Commandments

In the modern western world, the Ten Commandments are no longer regarded as the basis of morality. The rot set in many years ago when the Bible was subjected to destructive criticism. Inevitably, the foundations of the organised church were soon shaken. Not a few of the clergymen I have known regarded the Ten Commandments as largely irrelevant in today's society. Small wonder then, that the attitude is now common.

Take, for example, the third commandment: ' You shall not misuse the name of the LORD your God.' Or the fourth: 'Remember the Sabbath day, to keep it holy.' Both are openly violated and most people have no conscience about it. The seventh, 'You shall not commit adultery' is seen by some as the ultimate killjoy – a prohibition of legitimate pleasure.

Even among Christians, there is a lot of woolly thinking in this area. Some entertain the unsupportable notion that New Testament love makes the commandments redundant. Yet Jesus made it clear that he had not come to abolish the law: 'I tell you the truth, until heaven and earth disappear, not the smallest letter, not the least stroke of a pen, will by any means disappear from the Law until everything is accomplished' (Matt. 5:18). Not only this, but Jesus also added a new dimension to the commandments. 'You shall not murder' applies to hatred and 'You shall not commit adultery' forbids lust (Matt. 5:21,22,27,28).

Further support for the mistaken idea that Christians are no longer bound by the law is sought in Paul's words: '…you are not under law but under grace' (Rom. 6:14). But this means we are no longer under the condemnation of the law, which is a different matter. And, as the apostle explains, the commandments serve to bring sinners to realise their need of Christ: 'Indeed, I would not have known what sin was except through the law' (Rom. 7:7).

Whether we like it or not, the threefold application of the commandments still stands. First, in spite of wholesale abuse, they still serve to restrain sin and promote righteousness. Second, they are still the Spirit's instrument in convincing people of sin and of their need of Christ. Third – and this is relevant to our present purpose – they still stand as 'rules for living' for every saint.

Dead, but won't lie down

As we shall see in more detail later, there is a stubborn streak in our sinful nature that not only refuses to accept the authority of God's law but also reacts against it. It is not the fault of God's law, but of our own depravity. Why did I, as a child, deliberately walk on the grass when I saw the sign that told me to keep off it? Why does the young man in his first car put his foot down when he sees the speed restriction sign? Why do unruly teenagers refer to the police as 'pigs'?

The apostle Paul had the same problem: 'For I would not have known what coveting really was if the law had not said, "Do not covet." But sin, seizing the opportunity afforded by the commandment, produced in me every kind of covetous desire' (Rom. 7:7-8). The law of God is good, but our twisted sinful nature turns it into an occasion for sin.

Writing to the Colossians, the apostle says: 'Put to death, therefore, whatever belongs to your earthly nature: sexual immorality, impurity, lust, evil desires and greed, which is idolatry. Because of these, the wrath of God is coming. You used to walk in these ways, in the life you once lived. But now you must rid yourselves of all such things as these: anger, rage, malice, slander and filthy language from your lips (Col. 3:5-8).

The first three words 'put to death' puts the onus on the believer. He must mortify sin. But wait a minute – does not the same apostle tells us that we have already died to sin: 'Shall we go on sinning, so that grace may increase? By no means! We died to sin; how can we live in it any longer?' (Rom. 6:1-2).

What then, do we do with this contradiction? My first answer to this question, as to many similar questions, is this – the writer is not stupid. A highly intelligent man like Paul does not utter apparent contradictions unless there is a good reason for it. We have died to sin in the sense that sin shall not be our master any longer, because we are not under the law but under grace (Rom.

6:14). Sin no longer has any claim on our lives and our fight against it does not have an uncertain outcome. But, although the old sinful nature has received a mortal blow, it still rears its ugly head and will continue to do so as long as we are in this body.

I like the story of Mike, the headless chicken, who, it is claimed, lived for eighteen months after losing his top. Apparently, one night in March 1947, the headless Mike started choking in the middle of the night and died. Like the chicken, our old nature is still managing to run around, but it has no head and will soon die of its severe wounds! We could say the old nature is dead, but it will not lie down!

The saints' duty is to kill what is left of the chicken, but at the same time he must work on the principle that the chicken is already dead. As Paul says, we are to count ourselves 'dead to sin but alive to God in Christ Jesus' (Rom. 6:11).

When a person is saved, he is, in a real sense, united with Christ in his death and resurrection. 'For we know that our old self was crucified with him so that the body of sin might be rendered powerless…' (Rom. 6:6 footnote; 'the body of sin' means the old sinful nature). The apostle goes on to say: 'Now if we died with Christ, we believe that we will also live with him. For we know that since Christ was raised from the dead, he cannot die again…' (Rom. 6:8-9).

So if Christ cannot die, the saint cannot die either. Christ's death has delivered us forever from the penalty and power of sin. Therefore, although the old sinful nature is constantly waging war against our new nature, preventing us from doing what we now desire, it poses no ultimate threat (Rom. 7:21-25).

What devices shall we use then to kill off the chicken? Men like Thomas Beckett (*c.* 1118-70), Archbishop of Canterbury, and Thomas More (1478-1535), the Lord Chancellor of England, tried to do it by wearing hair shirts. The shirts were made from camel hair and worn next to the skin to cause maximum discomfort. They could even be regarded as instruments of torture because the skin would become red raw. How such intelligent men could think that discomfort could mortify their sins is hard to understand.

What is the best way to kill anything? The best way to kill a plant, for example, is to deprive it of water and food. It is also the best way to kill a sin. If I have a problem with lust, for instance, I must not feed it by reading pornographic magazines or watching the sex channels on TV. If I have a craving for alcohol, I must not keep a bottle handy in the cupboard or go for a drink with my friends. We do not conquer temptation by walking into it.

Let no-one say the fight is easy! The fight against sin is long, hard and relentless. From time to time, we shall fail, and when we do, we must confess our sins without delay, for God 'is faithful and just and will forgive us our sins and purify us from all unrighteousness' (1 John 1:9). But the fact that we shall not always gain the victory must never be used as a reason to stop fighting. Nor should we take any credit to ourselves when a victory is won.

There will be times when our resolve weakens. This may be due to illness, the fierceness of a particular temptation, or some bitter disappointment that has robbed us of our confidence. At such times we may be tempted to neglect prayer, Bible-reading, fellowship and worship. People who want to be in good health build up their strength when they are fit and well and are, therefore, better able to cope with illness when it comes. I understand it is a good way of dealing with depression. In the same way, saints who make the maximum use of their opportunities to grow in grace in the good times will be better able to cope with the tough times.

The journey through the dark valley does not last forever. The longing after holiness that is implanted in the soul of every true saint will never weaken permanently. Our delight in the law of God (Rom. 7:22) will remain and grow, simply because our God is faithful to his promises.

God's example

Jesus is the only perfect pattern of holiness, virtue and obedience. We may find good examples of holy living in many past saints, but none was without flaws and failings. The testimony provided in the Scriptures concerning the life of Jesus Christ is unique: '… Christ suffered for you, leaving you an example, that you should follow in his steps. "He committed no sin, and no deceit was found in his mouth"' (1 Peter 2:21, 22). This is why he was the only one good enough to pay the price of our sins.

During my life I have known many saintly people whose example has had a powerful influence in my life. I think of a dear friend – I shall call him Pastor B – who was the minister of a local church and from time to time asked me to preach. I was still in my early twenties. He was kind, helpful, and dealt graciously with my lack of experience. He was a passionate preacher with a genuine love for people. He was also a man of prayer. I could not fault his life and inevitably, I looked up to him.

Many years later, I was in conversation with a man who was a member of the church where Pastor B was the minister. Naturally, I enquired about his health and his ministry. There was an awkward silence for a moment, and then the man said, choosing his words carefully, 'I am sorry to tell you that Pastor B got himself into a moral difficulty.' Nothing further was said and of course, I did not press my question. Nevertheless, it was a bitter blow. I do not know to this day what the moral difficulty was, and it is better that I remain ignorant on the subject.

Some readers may be shocked if I were to say that this is what holy men of God are like. There has never been a blemish-free saint! The verdict on the life of King David of Israel, a man after God's own heart, whose behaviour was an example to his followers, runs as follows: 'For David had done what was right in the eyes of the LORD and had not failed to keep any of the LORD's commands all the days of his life – except in the case of Uriah the Hittite' (1 Kings 15:5).

Uriah was the husband of Bathsheba, with whom David had committed adultery. The king's attempt to bring Uriah from the front, where the king's army were fighting the enemy, and to persuade him to sleep with his wife, failed. David gave order to his Commander-in-Chief to put Uriah in the front line and then retreat from him, leaving him exposed to enemy fire. He died of his wounds (2 Sam. 11 & 12). We shall come back to this story later.

Wherever we look, no one measures up to the standard set by Jesus. The power of his example stems from two facts. First, he did not come as an angel but took our nature upon him and suffered just as we do, and much more. Therefore 'we do not have a high priest who is unable to sympathise with our weaknesses, but we have one who has been tempted in every way, just as we are – yet was without sin' (Heb. 4:15). Second, deep and enduring love for his people was the motive for his perfect life just as it was for his perfect death. Jesus himself said so in his prayer to his father: 'For them I sanctify myself, that they too may be truly sanctified' (John 17:19).

My children used to wear what were called WWJD wristbands. The letters stand for 'What would Jesus do?' The idea was that the wristbands would remind them to think before taking action in any particular situation. I am pleased to say that my children would have been more competent to answer the question than many children would of their age.

It is at this point that so many of us are deficient. We do not spend time reading the Gospels and contemplating Christ's moral example and, therefore, we do not always know how Jesus would act in a given set of circumstances.

9. God's Word

The saints' guide

About twenty-seven years ago, when I was the Rector of Chadwell St Mary in Essex, I fell sick and was confined to bed. A boy in the Sunday School, about nine or ten years old, drew a cartoon of me lying in bed trying to pick up my Bible which was just out of reach! I am not sure what point he was making, but if he intended to depict my frustration at not being able read the Word of God he had understanding beyond his years.

The words of Job are a challenge to every saint: 'I have treasured the words of his mouth more than my daily bread' (Job 23:12). Judging by recent surveys, many believers would not feel deprived if the Scriptures were taken away from them for a whole week or more. But they would not be prepared to go without food for that length of time.

This is precisely what the Israelites had to suffer to learn that God's Word to the children of God is every bit as important as their daily food. We read in Exodus chapter 16:1-3 that they complained bitterly about the lack of food. Moses told them, God 'humbled you, causing you to hunger and then feeding you with manna, which neither you nor your fathers had known, to teach you that man does not live on bread alone but on every word that comes from the mouth of the Lord' (Deut. 8:3).

The importance of the Word of God to our growth in holiness is obvious. Our appetite for it is a reliable indicator of the strength of our desire to be like Jesus. The Psalmist was well aware of it: 'I have hidden your word in my heart that I might not sin against you' (Ps. 119:11). Only by frequent reading of the Word are we able to hide it in our hearts. The only way to hide it in our hearts is to read it. God does not bring to mind the relevant portion of his Word when the need arises, if it has not been written there previously. Knowledge of the Scriptures will sharpen our discernment as to what pleases God as nothing else can.

It is this kind of devotion to the Scriptures that provokes the unspiritual man to accuse us of bibliolatry (worship of the Bible). The criticism is totally without foundation and exposes the ignorance of those who make it. We do not bow down to paper and ink even when it is used to print the Word, but to the Lord whose Word it is.

At the church at which my wife and I worship every Sunday, I notice that the musicians sometimes put their Bibles on the floor when they are playing their instruments. They do the same with their music. Some would argue that this is showing disrespect for the Word of God. But I happen to know that those musicians love God's Word. They also know that there is a big difference between honouring the Word of God on the one hand, and showing respect for the paper and ink on the other.

I have accidentally dropped my Bible many times. I have sat on it, torn it, spilt coffee and communion wine on it. Surely, any book in daily use is bound to suffer in this way. In any case, pages that are regularly thumbed start to fray at the edges. A well-worn Bible tells me a lot about its owner.

The Bible and holiness

The saints should never underestimate the vital role the Bible plays in their sanctification. Without it, they would be helpless. Jesus tells us why. In his prayer to his Father, he prays for his disciples who are alive in this world (John 17:20). The burden of his prayer, as any reading of the seventeenth chapter of John's Gospel will show, is that true believers may be protected, sanctified, united and glorified.

But how would we know about these things? How are we to be made aware of these blessings? Jesus was not in doubt: 'Sanctify them by the truth; your word is truth' (John 17:17). If this is the substance of the prayer of Christ for his church as is clearly the case, how can we be in any doubt about the importance of the Bible in our lives?

How can we be in any doubt that the Word of God is the Holy Spirit's tool for making the saints holy? 'The word of God is living and active. Sharper than any double-edged sword, it penetrates even to dividing soul and spirit, joints and marrow; it judges the thoughts and attitudes of the heart' (Heb. 4:12). Just as the surgeon's knife cuts through the body to get to the organ that needs repairing, so the Word cuts deep into our souls to reveal those sins that need cutting out.

Psalm 119 is a classic on this subject. It reveals the Psalmist's delight in God's holy Word: 'Your statues are my delight; they are my counsellors' (verse 24). 'Direct me in the paths of your commands, for there I find delight' (verse 35). 'The law from your mouth is more precious to me than thousands of pieces of silver and gold' (verse 72). 'Oh, how I love your law! I meditate on it all day long' (verse 97).

Surely, the guidance the Scriptures provide on holy living is one of the reasons why the Psalmist loved them. 'How can a young man keep his way pure? By living according to your word' (verse 9). 'I have chosen the way of truth; I have set my heart on your laws' (verse 30). Saints who fail at this point will be stunted in their growth. They will be far less likely to conquer temptation and to establish a Biblical code of practice.

When Jesus identified God's Word with truth, he did not mean that nothing else is true, but that the Scriptures are truth in a special way. In particular, they are truth about the way of salvation. This is why we refer to them as 'the truth'.

John 17:19 comes as a surprise: 'For them I sanctify myself, that they too may be truly sanctified.' We want to ask why a perfect Jesus needs to be sanctified. The only possible meaning is that Jesus is using the word 'sanctify' in the sense of being set apart. He was set apart so that we too may be set apart. He was set apart so that by his death, he redeemed his people from the consequences of their sins, and set them on the road to holiness in preparation for the glory to come.

He gave himself up to make the church holy, 'cleansing her by the washing with water through the word, and to present her to himself as a radiant church, without stain or wrinkle or any other blemish' (Eph:5:26). Therefore, Christ separated (sanctified) himself so that he might also separate (sanctify) the church. Paul's mention of water is almost certainly a reference to the symbolism of baptism.

Practical application

Sanctification is very practical. I am reminded of the words of Mary, the Mother of Jesus, to the servants at the wedding in Cana: 'Do whatever he tells you' (John 2:5). Blessed thoughts are not much good if they do not translate into action. We must not only know the truth but also obey it. 'My food', said Jesus, 'is to do the will of him who sent me and to finish his work' (John 4:34). Again, in John 6:38, 'For I have come down from heaven not to do my will but to do the will of him who sent me.' This is the pattern for every saint, as John explains: 'Whoever claims to live in him must walk as Jesus did' (1 John 2:6). If meditation does not lead to action, it is mere day-dreaming.

I must stress yet again, that this is not a demand for perfection. Perfect obedience, as in the case of Jesus, is perfect sanctification, and is unattainable in this life. The apostle John himself reminds us that 'If we claim to be without sin, we deceive ourselves and the truth is not in us' (1 John 1:8). Nevertheless, it is the standard we are to aim at.

I remember being challenged by a woman who was very young in the faith. She complained that I did not show any pleasure whenever she told me that someone had been converted to Christ. The words of John immediately came to mind and I read them to her: 'It has given me great joy to find some of your children walking in the truth, just as the Father commanded us' (2 John 4). Professions of faith often turn out to be false, but the evidence of change in a new convert's life is a real cause for rejoicing.

Here are some of the ways in which the Spirit of God uses the Word of God to achieve holy living in the believer. I do not put them in particular order, although the portrayal of Jesus Christ as the supreme example of a holy life must come high in the order of importance. The cure for the view that holiness has primarily to do with not causing offence and making compromises for the sake of peace, is to read the Gospels.

It is through the 'great and precious promises' God gives that we 'participate in the divine nature and escape the corruption in the world caused by evil desires' (2 Peter 1:3). Through the Word, we have new life from above and are no longer under the power of sin. The chains that held us in a state of depravity have fallen off and we are free to serve the Lord.

The Scriptures provide us with a map that shows us the way to heaven. Indeed, we could see them as a satellite navigation device, 'For we are God's workmanship, created in Christ Jesus to do good works, which God prepared in advance for us to do' (Eph. 2:10). God prepared our pathway long before we knew anything of the new birth.

Far from being robots, it is now our responsibility to discover God's plan and purpose for our lives. To do this, we must take Paul's directive seriously: 'Let the word of Christ dwell in you richly as you teach and admonish one another with all wisdom…' (Col. 3:16).

We may divide the task into two parts. First, no matter what our training or our occupation may be, our first priority is to discover how we should behave in our daily lives. The Bible provides instructions galore on how to conduct ourselves towards our wives, our children, our superiors and those who are lower down the social ladder. We have guidance on how to behave in the home, the church, society, and how to treat our neighbour, our pastor and our fellow-believers.

The second part is to try to discover what God wants us to do with our lives and our talents. This is much more difficult. But no saint should assume that there is no specific task for him to accomplish. As the old hymn says, 'There's a work for Jesus none but you can do.' But neither should he contemplate serving the church either at home or overseas if he is not making significant progress in shedding the filthy garments of the old life.

Obviously, the Scriptures only give indirect help on the matter of personal vocation. However, the more our lives are enriched by the Word, the better able we shall be to discern the will of God in this matter. Biblical illiteracy gives rise to foolish decisions.

An ever-increasing knowledge of God's Word will also help us keep our consciences clear and tender so that any sin in our lives is immediately brought to light and dealt with. Some sins will prove difficult to handle, but when victory is not immediately achieved, our knowledge of Scripture will help us to go on fighting. The Holy Spirit will never let saints remain happy in sin and will bring relevant verses to mind.

Recently I was in the waiting room at the local health centre. The opposite wall was full of posters and notices. One caught my eye. It depicted a pile of cigarette ends with the caption: 'Never give up giving up.' It reminded me of one of my mother's favourite sayings: 'If at first you don't succeed, try, try and try again.' Those whose minds are saturated with the Scriptures will find it harder to give up fighting sin. We are back to the Psalmist's reason for hiding God's Word in his heart – 'that I might not sin against you'.

Spending time with Jesus

'Martha, Martha… you are worried about many things, but only one thing is needed. Mary has chosen what is better, and it will not be taken away from her' (Luke 10:41-42). Why did Jesus deliver this gentle yet pointed rebuke to Martha? Both Martha and her sister Mary were close friends of Jesus.

One day, when Martha had kindly opened her home to Jesus and his disciples, she became irritated by her sister who, instead of helping in the kitchen, sat at the feet of Jesus listening to what he said. When Martha could stand it no longer, she came to Jesus and said: 'Lord, don't you care that my sister has left me to do the work by myself? Tell her to help me!' (Luke 10:40).

The rebuke followed. What did it mean? Why had Mary chosen what was better? Was Jesus encouraging her to be lazy and inconsiderate? Not at all. The fact is, Mary had recognised a golden opportunity to hear the teaching of Jesus and she took full advantage of it. She was not going to allow the work of entertaining guests to interfere.

The rebuke implied that Martha should have been sitting with her sister at the Master's feet. Being hospitable to an honourable guest is commendable, but on this occasion Jesus would have preferred Martha to sit with her sister at his feet.

The lesson is surely this – not merely that we should not allow our worries to get on top of us, but also that we should get our priorities right. In our situation it means that to spend time listening to God speaking through his Word must take precedence over our service. Christians who dash around like scalded cats from one task to another, leaving no time to spend with the Word of God, are guilty of Martha's sin. On the other hand, those who follow the example of Mary here will find that they cope much better with the 'worries' of daily life. As I look back over my life, I cannot help wishing I had paid more attention to this matter.

The fight against sin

The saints' constant fight is against the world, the flesh and the devil. Remember, the 'world' means the domain of Satan, 'the prince of this world' (John 12:31) with his hostility against God and his saints. The 'flesh' simply refers to the sinful nature that is in all of us. The Scriptures must figure prominently in our fight against all three adversaries.

For this reason alone, we have to encourage one another to resist the temptation to be lazy in our reading of the Word. So many pressures are on us to abandon it. The notion of absolute truth – truth that is the same for everyone – is widely rejected in our society. We are facing an illogical but widespread philosophy – that there is no such thing as the truth, because truth is different for each person. I have my truth and you have your truth, but my truth is not the same as your truth.

According to this philosophy, I no longer have any right to say you are wrong and you have no right to tell me I am wrong. I have to respect your truth because it is true for you. The possibility that one of us may be wrong is no longer on the agenda. What we are up against is this – the word 'truth' has lost its meaning.

Now it is obvious that, taken to its logical conclusion, this becomes ridiculous. If what I believe is false, how can it be true for me? If, for example, I believe I can live without eating and drinking, I am wrong and I shall die. This is a universal truth. If I believe I can shoot you dead with a banana, it would be easy to prove that I am wrong.

If there were no such thing as absolute universal truth, life would be impossible. That such a philosophy is now accepted in our 'sophisticated' society betrays our stupidity. The fact remains that an atmosphere is created in which belief in the absolute truth of God's Word is seen as offensive.

Amid the cacophony of opposing voices, the words of Jesus sound loud and clear. Speaking to his Father, he said, 'Your word is truth' (John 17:17) – not just truth for you or truth for me, but truth for everybody. Speaking to unbelieving Jews, Jesus said, 'The Scripture cannot be broken' (John 10:35). No matter what the critics say, the truth of God stands.

I have no wish to tone down the seriousness of the present situation, but I believe that the ever-changing views about truth highlight the importance of living the truth. It is very difficult for unbelievers to deny the evidence of a transformed life. We must never be ashamed of God's truth. Whatever strange ideas come into vogue, the Spirit will continue to apply the Word so that it breaks down the barriers set up by godless philosophies and achieves the purpose God intends (Isa. 55:11).

Speaking to believing Jews, Jesus taught that 'the truth will set you free' (John 8:32). Those who believe the Scriptures are set free from the burden of sin and guilt. They are set free from the condemnation of God's law. There are no such freedoms to be had by believing 'your truth' or 'my truth'. Freedom is only to be found in 'the truth'. All this means that truth about God, truth about judgment, truth about the way of salvation and so on, is revealed by God and is not up for debate. It carries his authority. Let us then resist every temptation to neglect the reading and study of the Word, as many are now doing.

As well as the ongoing temptation to read the Word in a superficial manner so that it does not sink down into the heart, it is still possible to be well versed in Scripture and still ignore it. This is a fight against the enemy within. Obviously, it is of the greatest concern to us in a book on sanctification. To understand the nature of this battle, we need to consider Paul's words carefully: 'So I find this law at work: When I want to do good, evil is right there with me' (Rom. 7:21). The apostle is telling us that he has to fight a constant battle between his 'inner being' (his new nature from God) and his old nature. Every saint suffers in this way.

In the next verse we learn that the Scriptures intensify the conflict: 'For in my inner being I delight in God's law; but I see another law at work in the members of my body, waging war against the law of my mind and making me a prisoner of the law of sin at work within my members' (Rom. 7:22-23). The new Paul takes sheer delight in God's law but he is keenly aware of an opposing principle that he also calls a law. This is the old sinful nature still asserting itself.

The discerning reader of the entire passage (Rom. 7:14-25) will see that Paul uses the pronoun 'I' to refer both to his old sinful nature and also to his new nature. It is almost as if he is having a dialogue with himself. We could paraphrase it like this: 'When I (the new Paul) want to be obedient to God's law which I love, I (the old Paul) want to be disobedient to it, which I (the new Paul) hate.' Although he thanks God for ultimate victory in verse 25a, he makes it perfectly clear in verse 25b, that the fight will go on as long as he is in this body.

The regular reading of the Scriptures with prayer is therefore vital if we are to gain victory over the tendency of the old nature to break the law. If we really love God whose Word it is, we shall not disobey, at least not without prompt repentance. Of course, the less we read it, the less we shall love it and the more inclined we shall become to be content with our ignorance. Nothing is more detrimental to our growth in personal holiness.

I have no hesitation in saying that the attainment of gospel holiness is impossible unless we have confidence in the authority of the Bible and if we are not regularly consulting it and submitting to its claims. How can we even talk about obedience to Christ if we do not read or believe what he says? The commandments, the promises, the apostolic teaching, the example of the Lord Jesus, are to be found in the Bible and nowhere else. Indeed, there is no aspect of sanctification that is not related to God's Word. To get rid of the Bible is to say goodbye to holiness.

10. God's witnesses

The saints' task

Holiness beautifies the gospel

'In everything set them an example by doing what is good. In your teaching show integrity, seriousness and soundness of speech that cannot be condemned, so that those who oppose you may be ashamed because they have nothing bad to say about us' (Titus 2:7-8). Paul is writing to Titus. It is important to notice the order of the apostle instructions. 'Soundness of speech' counts for nothing if it is not supported by integrity.

Many years ago, when I was in the retail business, I engaged a Christian who had some experience in the trade. I shall call her Miss M Barrass. I soon discovered that she was outspoken about her faith. In a very short time, all the members of staff knew what she believed. I did not complain about this, but soon things began to go wrong. When I returned from the bank one morning, she had gathered the rest of the staff around her and was, in her words 'witnessing to them'. They all had work to do and, in any case, it would not have been very appropriate for a customer to walk in and see the staff in a huddle!

Talking with Miss Barrass later, in private, it became clear that she thought I would be pleased. I cannot remember the exact conversation, but I pointed out to her that there is a time and place for verbal witness and that she had chosen neither the right time nor the right place. I cannot imagine what would have happened if one of the directors had walked in.

Things did not improve. She began arriving late for work and when I chided her for it, she began to arrive on time but then went straight to the staff room to powder her nose and put her lipstick on. Then her fifteen-minute coffee break began to stretch to twenty minutes, and then twenty-five minutes. The rest of the staff were not slow to notice. When I tackled her about this, she said she had been praying. We had reached the point where she was becoming an embarrassment.

Need I say that the members of staff were not impressed? They complained to me that Miss Barrass did not pull her weight. Their observations reminded me of the old jibe, 'What you are shouts so loudly I cannot hear what you say.' Unbelievers may be blind to spiritual truth and helpless in the matter of their eternal welfare, but they are very efficient in detecting hypocrisy. They smell it a mile away!

Making the gospel attractive is every saint's calling. To achieve it we must practise righteousness and fair play. We must be down to earth and show concern and consideration for others. We must be able to present ourselves as an example of what God can do with sinners. If we set a good example, we may cause some to glorify God. If bad, we may cause them to blaspheme his holy Name. Where the good example is lacking, 'witnessing' is more likely to achieve the latter.

The saint must never say that a higher standard of behaviour is something he cannot attain. He must never say, 'This habit is my weakness and I cannot help it.' In the light of God's grace, none of the old habits may be seen as permanent. Sin must not be his master.

Holiness commends God's Word

Some say that the church leader's moral standard must be higher than that of church members. Not too long ago, the bishops of the

Church of England drew up a ridiculous proposal that homosexual ministers should be allowed to live with their boyfriends as long as they gave an assurance that they would abstain from 'sex'! No such proposal was put forward for members of the congregation. It is true of course, that the sins of pastors are more likely to hit the headlines. Paul is adamant, however, that the behaviour of all Christian men and women is just as important.

Titus was a Christian minister! Paul tells him to 'Teach the older men to be temperate, worthy of respect, self-controlled, and sound in faith, in love and in endurance.' Pastor Titus must also 'Teach the older women to be reverent in the way they live, not to be slanderers or addicted to much wine, but to teach what is good'. Then they in turn will be able to train the younger women 'to love their husbands and children, to be self-controlled and pure, to be busy at home, to be kind, and to be subject to their husbands...' (Titus 2:1-5).

Paul's purpose in this passage was to ensure 'that no-one will malign the word of God' (verse 5). Maligning the Word of God is no less serious than blaspheming the name of God. He is just as jealous over his holy Word as he is over his holy name. We believe that what Scripture says, God says. In Rom. 9:17 we read that 'the Scripture says to Pharaoh: "I raised you up for this very purpose, that I might display my power in you..." which is just the same as saying, 'God says to Pharaoh'.

Blaspheming God's name

Blasphemy is serious. The abolition of blasphemy laws by any government does not alter the fact. The commandment prohibiting blasphemy stands for all time and for all circumstances: 'You shall not misuse the name of the LORD your God, for the LORD will not hold anyone guiltless who misuses his name' (Exod. 20:7).

There can be no doubt about the meaning of this. Where there is no sincere repentance, the person who uses the name of God in any of its forms in a careless or irreverent manner will not escape severe punishment. What do we say then about people who claim to be Christians whose bad behaviour causes others to blaspheme? The Old Testament prophets Isaiah and Ezekiel complained in their day about the bad behaviour of the Jews because it caused pagans to blaspheme God's name. Paul echoes their verdict in his condemnation of the behaviour of the Jews in the first century: 'God's name is blasphemed among the Gentiles because of you' (Rom. 2:24). Things have not changed.

Careful reading of the context shows that the Jews were proud of God's law and considered themselves able instructors of the foolish and proficient teachers of infants. They preached against stealing, adultery and idolatry and yet were guilty of all three (Rom. 2:17-23). Paul challenges them with some searching questions: 'You who preach against stealing, do you steal? You who say that people should not commit adultery, do you commit adultery? …You who brag about the law, do you dishonour God by breaking the law?' (Rom. 2:21-23). At the same time as they were bragging about the law of God, they were bringing reproach on his name by their inexcusable conduct.

Now it would be rather foolish to suggest that every Jew was guilty. No doubt, some avoided these offences. Similarly, it would be equally foolish to assume that all privileged Gentiles have been guilty. Nevertheless, many who profess Christ are guilty of shaming his name by their appalling behaviour.

In our own land, people of other faiths are rejecting the Christian message because they see a huge gap between the profession and practice of people who claim to be Christians. Admittedly, they falsely assume that people are Christians just because they live in a country with a Christian heritage. They do not have the ability to distinguish between nominal and genuine believers. Even so, the damage is incalculable.

Shining like stars

Every living thing on this earth depends on the sun for physical light and life. Without the sun, we would all die. Every human being on this earth depends on Christ for spiritual light and life. Without him, spiritual and eternal death are inevitable. Jesus is 'the light of the world' (John 8:12) in several ways. In the Scriptures, light stands for God's holiness (1 Tim. 6:16), God's favour (2 Cor. 4:6) and God's revelation.

Once we understand this, we get a better grasp of what Jesus meant. He did not claim to be *a* light but *the* light. He is not one of many lights in the world, but the only light. We must not water this down. Human beings who are physically alive but do not know Christ, exist in a state of spiritual death no matter what else they believe.

Jesus also taught us that the saints are 'the light of the world'. This is a bombshell! The context shows that when Jesus made this astonishing statement in the Sermon on the Mount, he was talking about good deeds. Christian disciples are to be seen doing good, not for self-praise but to cause others to praise God. 'A city on a hill cannot be hidden. Neither do people light a lamp and put it under a bowl. Instead they put it on its stand, and it gives light to everyone in the house. In the same way, let your light shine before men, that they may see your good deeds and praise your Father in heaven' (Matt. 5:14-16).

Luke tells us how Paul exercised this ministry. He was sent by Jesus to open the eyes of the Gentiles and 'turn them from darkness to light, and from the power of Satan to God, so that they may receive forgiveness of sin and a place among those who are sanctified by faith in me' (Acts 26:18). So Paul, like his Master, was 'a light for revelation to the Gentiles and for glory to your people Israel' (Luke 2:32).

Some nights, when I go to bed and the sky is clear, I do not switch on the light or draw the curtains. I walk to the window, look up at the stars and stand amazed. Nor does my amazement ever wane. Indeed, the more I do it, the more wonderful it seems. These apparently tiny sources of light are so numerous it is impossible to count them. Some are so far away, it takes thousands of years for their light to reach the earth. Some, we are told, are ten thousand times brighter than the sun.

More often than not at such times, I am reminded of the words of the Psalmist: 'The heavens declare the glory of God; the skies proclaim the work of his hands. Day after day they pour forth speech; night after night they display knowledge. There is no speech or language where their voice is not heard. Their voice goes out into all the earth, their words to the ends of the world' (Ps. 19:1-4).

How appropriate it is that Paul should use similar words to describe the proclamation of the gospel. Not that the Psalmist intended to convey this meaning, but there is an obvious parallel between the revelation of God in nature and in Scripture. Light has always been a synonym for truth. After urging us to do everything without complaint or arguing, so that we may become blameless and pure, children of God without fault in a crooked and depraved generation, the apostle adds these words: 'in which you shine like stars in the universe as you hold out the word of life…' (Phil 2:14-16).

Just as the stars in the night sky declare the glory of God, so the saints glorify God in bringing the light of the gospel in word and deed to this benighted world. Of course, the stars do not speak. They reveal the glory of God by what they are. The well-known saying, 'actions speak louder than words' was not used in the time of Jesus and the apostles, but they certainly understood the principle.

There is, of course, a time to speak. There is no support in Scripture for those who say there is no need to say anything as long as our lives speak for God. Indeed, Peter tells us that we should 'Always be prepared to give an answer to everyone who asks you to give the reason for the hope that you have' (1 Peter

3:15). The point to be stressed is this – our words must be backed up by a holy life. If this is not the case, it would be better to keep our mouths shut!

Within the first few weeks of taking up a new ministry, I was warned by several people in the church to beware of Norman Briggs (not his real name). I filed the information in my mental pending file. As time passed it became obvious that Norman was being criticised because his commitment to the life of the church put his critics to shame. Anything bad they had to say about him turned out to be untrue. If his critics were not ashamed, then they ought to have been.

The situation worsened when Norman was converted. It is not an exaggeration to say that some of his critics were furious because now, Norman, for the first time in his life, was not ashamed to speak of his Saviour and took great delight in God's Word. His detractors did not like it one bit. Most of them had known Norman all his life and they now tried to accuse him of betraying them by taking things too far. His blameless life eventually put them to silence.

The test of love

How vital it is then, to make sure that living to honour God is of first importance in our lives. Although it demands discipline and effort, it is not attainable without a deep and abiding love for the Lord Jesus. Such love grows deeper the more we understand the depth of his love for us. With this love comes an ever-increasing sense of gratitude to God for what he has done for us. And since gratitude is an incentive to holiness, it follows that as it increases, so does the power of the incentive.

It is not difficult to determine how fervent our love for Christ really is. All we have to do is to put two questions to ourselves. Jesus himself lays down the first and most important test: 'If you

love me,' he said, 'you will obey what I command' (John 14:15).
The question therefore is this: 'How eager am I to read, understand,
and obey Christ's commands?'

The second and closely linked question is this: How fervently
do I love my brother?' I say it is closely linked because if we do
not love our brother, it proves that we do not love God either. As
the apostle John points out, 'If anyone says, "I love God," yet
hates his brother, he is a liar. For anyone who does not love his
brother, whom he has seen, cannot love God, whom he has not
seen' (1 John 4:20).

The second question, therefore, is really part of the first, but
I call attention to it separately because all too often lovelessness
spoils the fellowship and witness of the church. It is a good exercise
to sit down and identify in your mind the person you love least in
your fellowship. You may safely conclude that your love for Christ
is no greater than your love for that person. I sometimes wonder
how we can sing hymns and songs about loving Jesus when there
is bitterness in our hearts against someone. We shall come back to
this important subject in the next chapter.

A member of a Bible-Study group of which I was the leader,
once said to me: 'You are giving us too much elementary teaching
and we need to move on.' If you should be thinking along these
lines as you read, let me give you the same reply I gave to that
person so many years ago: 'No one moves out of the elementary
stage in this subject until there is evidence that real progress is
being made in the practice of loving one another.'

Moreover, where this is not the case, growth in holiness is bound
to be stunted. Love for Christ and love for our brothers and sisters
in Christ is a permanent and basic essential in our walk with God.
Failure at this point dishonours the Son and 'he who does not honour
the Son does not honour the Father who sent him' (John 5:23).

Every saint then is called to be the light of the world. He is
called, not to advertise his own virtues, but to live for the glory of
God. He must indeed be constantly moving forward in holy living

without forgetting the basics. The more holy he becomes, the more telling his words will be.

Don't tell me, show me

When I was younger, I did almost all my own car maintenance and repairs. In those days, there were no mysteries under the bonnet as there are today. I would either buy or borrow a manual for my particular car make and model and read the appropriate instructions. Sometimes, in spite of the illustrations and diagrams, I had difficulty in understanding the procedures and, as a result, I wondered if the job might be beyond my ability.

What a difference it made when I was privileged to watch someone else do the job. Seeing the components 'in the flesh' and watching how they were dismantled gave me all the confidence I needed. The task no longer seemed beyond my capability.

I am not suggesting that the instructions in the Scriptures on how to live a holy life are hard to understand. The point I am making is this – it is better to show others by example how to live the Christian life than to tell them how to do it. As I said earlier, when it is appropriate, it makes good sense to do both, but if I am unable to show others how to do it, it would be better to keep quiet.

Let us take care then that we show the love that will endorse our words. Jesus said 'All men will know that you are my disciples, if you love one another' (John 13:35). If there is no love between us, the unbelieving observer will come to a very different conclusion.

Humility and a clean mouth

Readers for whom English is a second language would probably not understand the two following idioms without explanation. To say someone is a 'down-to-earth' person is a compliment because it describes someone who is realistic and straightforward. He is not pretentious or affected in any way. On the other hand, to say that a person is 'toffee-nosed' means that he thinks of himself as superior to others. His attitude and his speech make it clear that he regards others, especially the lower social classes, with contempt.

A few weeks before I went to college to train for the ministry, two men were repairing the brick pillars that supported the gates in front of my garage. I went out with two cups of tea and shouted, 'tea up'. My neighbour, who was gardening, overheard what I said. She stood to her feet and called over the fence in a disapproving voice, 'You'll never be a bishop talking like that.'

In the first place, I could not understand why she should assume that I wanted to be a bishop. But nor could I identify with her reasoning about my language. Why should she expect a clergyman to avoid everyday language? What, I wonder, did she expect me to say? I am quite sure the two workmen did not regard the two words 'tea up' as being crude or vulgar.

But to speak or act in a manner that is 'toffee-nosed', as if we consider 'ordinary' people as being beneath us and therefore do not want to be associated with them, is entirely out of place for the saints. Prejudice has nothing to do with sanctification.

Being down-to-earth however, has everything to do with it. It does not mean being vulgar. Not just ministers, but all believers have a duty to obey Paul's command: 'Do not let any unwholesome talk come out of your mouths, but only what is helpful for building others up according to their needs, that it may benefit those who listen' (Eph. 4:29). We do not use foul language. Nor do we take part in impure conversation.

I learned from a recent issue of 'Evangelicals Now' about a pastor in America known as the 'Cussing Preacher'. 'Cussing' is American slang for swearing. Apparently, he presents the gospel clearly in his preaching but regularly uses 'colourful language'. He also encourages gambling and borderline movies in his church.

Yet, so it is claimed, he is able to reach out to his 'post-modern' neighbourhood.

The first question that arises in my mind is this: Does this kind of activity conform to the pattern set by Jesus himself? We know that Jesus was not afraid to mix with prostitutes and fraudulent tax-gatherers. He was not afraid of getting his hands dirty. He came from the glory of the highest place to the degradation of the lowest, a distance far greater than any of us can conceive. But he remained pure.

Nor did he compromise his position in any way by what came out of his mouth. People 'were amazed at the gracious words that came from his lips' (Luke 4:22). He was in the world, yet not of the world, untainted by his closeness to the immoral and the self-righteous of society. No one could prove him guilty of sin (John 8:46). Now if the one who is our supreme example did not sin with his lips, what warrant have we to do so? The notion that being 'one of the boys' helps us to get alongside them is a serious blunder. There is no place for 'cussing preachers' or cussing saints in this school and, happily, it is reported that the man described above has changed his ways.

11. God's church

The saints' privilege

The testimony of a holy fellowship

'The world has yet to see what God can do with a man fully consecrated to him. By God's help, I aim to be that man.' Although there is some doubt about the origin of these well-known words, they are usually attributed to Dwight L. Moody, the American evangelist.

Why, I wonder, did he confine it to one man? May we not better say 'the world has yet to see what God can do with a church fully consecrated to him'? I guess most believers would think such an achievement is impossible. If it were possible, it would certainly be more effective than the consecration of one individual because the world would have the advantage of watching how Christians love one another and work together in harmony.

But just as Judas Iscariot was a member of Christ's inner circle, so there will always be pseudo-believers in the church. Since we cannot see into the heart, membership of the church down here cannot be based on anything other than a credible profession of faith. The infallible separation of the tares and the wheat must await the appropriate time: 'Let both grow together until the harvest. At that time I will tell the harvesters: "First collect the weeds and tie them in bundles to be burned, then gather the wheat and bring it into my barn' (Matt. 13:30).

At least we should all follow Paul's example. He aimed at the full maturity of every member: 'We proclaim him, admonishing and teaching everyone with all wisdom, so that we may present everyone perfect in Christ. To this end I labour, struggling with all his energy, which so powerfully works in me' (Col. 1:28-29).

One body, many members

The ability of my computer to remember and manoeuvre millions of bits of information around never ceases to amaze me. Yet, it cannot compare with the human brain, which sends billions of bits of information round the body. It provides automatic focus and aperture adjustment to the eyes so that we see clearly. It interprets the sounds received from our ears. It co-ordinates our movement and the functions of the body we seldom even think about, like breathing. And all this in a lump of fat about three pounds in weight – a bit lighter than my computer!

The human body, of which the brain is the control centre, is also an exceedingly complex machine. It has an incredible ability to heal itself when damage occurs. The skeleton on which it is built has hinges and joints that are self-lubricating. Every minute, the heart pumps over a gallon of blood through thousands of miles of blood vessels. Our organs turn food into energy and living tissue. We even have a 'thermostat' that controls our body temperature with a very efficient alarm system when we are getting too hot or too cold.

Why then, I wonder, am I so amazed at my computer? I think my amazement stems from the fact that God has given such ability to human beings to create something so complex. On the other hand, maybe it has something to do with my over-familiarity with the marvels of creation.

Another organism amazes me even more. God created it and he maintains it. Unlike my computer and my human body, it is indestructible. It is under constant attack from all quarters and yet the amazing thing about it is that God cooperates with his people in keeping it functioning.

I speak of the creation and continuity of the church – 'the body of Christ' as Paul calls it. Here we have a living organism (not an organisation) that goes back to the time of Abraham and takes its final shape through the once-for-all-time sacrifice of Christ and the ongoing work of the Spirit in the calling of the elect.

The church is indestructible because Jesus has guaranteed that even 'the gates of Hades will not overcome it' (Matt. 16:9b). Of course, this does not mean that denominations are not expendable. The true church consists of those whom God has called and is calling out of this world; those whom Christ purchased with his blood 'from every tribe and language and people and nation' (Rev. 5:9). The Greek word for 'church' in the New Testament is *ekklesia*, which comes from the verb *ekkaleo*, to call out. This is made up of two words – *ek*, out of, and *kaleo*, to call. The saints are called out of the world to belong to God's universal family.

The church of God transcends all human barriers, so that the holy fellowship of the saints is a foretaste of heaven itself. Peter describes her as 'a chosen people, a royal priesthood, a holy nation, a people belonging to God' (1 Peter 2:9). It is important to notice that the nouns are all collective – people, priesthood and nation. Indeed, the emphasis in the Scriptures is on the corporate nature of the church. The saints belong to God and to each other.

God appointed Christ to be 'head over everything for the church, which is his body...' (Eph. 1:22-23). Just as the head controls the body, so Christ as head presides over the church, his body. The Spirit of Christ – the Holy Spirit – lives in every member and in the body as a whole. We all – that is, every saint – depend on him for life and growth, and we depend on each other for mutual encouragement and support. Just as 'the body is a unit, though it is made up of many parts…' (1 Cor. 12:12), so the church is one body with many inter-dependent parts.

Paul describes this inter-dependence in a rather humorous way: 'The eye cannot say to the hand, "I don't need you!" And the head cannot say to the feet, "I don't need you!"…But God has combined the members of the body… so that there should be no division in the body, but that its parts should have equal concern for each other' (1 Cor. 12:21,22,24,25).

Saints in any place are, of course, mainly concerned with the local church of which they are members. It is, or should be, the local expression of a worldwide fellowship. This is one of the principal places where we learn to grow in holiness.

'Ah, but', someone will say, 'there is not much harmony in my local church. The pastor cannot preach and doesn't visit. Very few people go and they are always quarrelling among themselves. Some attend regularly and others only when they are free from other "obligations" like parties and football matches.'

The existence of such 'churches' creates a problem for newly born saints and regular attendance at one is likely to hinder their spiritual development. Most young converts in my experience assumed that the saints would be found in every church building and that every minister preaches the gospel. I always advised them to avoid dead churches like the plague – and I did it with a clear conscience.

Many years ago, on holiday with my wife, we went to the local church for morning worship. I guess there would be about forty people present in a building that would have seated several hundred. There was nothing Christian about the songs we were asked to sing, no reading from the Bible, and the subject of the 'sermon' was 'How the Union Jack was formed.'

Part way through the 'sermon' I was so disgusted I was inclined to walk out, but my wife was sitting on the end of the row. Knowing her as I do, I felt she would consider it rather rude so I decided to grin and bear it. Suddenly, to my surprise and relief, she got up and said 'let's go'. I can assure the reader that for my wife to do something like that, she would have to be more than disgusted with the proceedings.

I have no hesitation in saying that this was not a church at all in the biblical sense of the word. The Spirit of Christ dwells only in true believers who love to worship Christ and to be together. They do not settle for sermons on how we got the Union Jack. God does not dwell in the hearts of people just because they attend a 'church' building or become members of a failed organisation. He does not even dwell in those who have been baptised if it was a matter of just going through the ritual. Nor does he dwell in the hearts of ministers just because they have been ordained or appointed to an office in the church. No matter what a person's status may be, if he does not love Jesus Christ and his Holy Word, he is a stranger to the grace of God.

Corporate sanctification

Whether we like it or not, belonging to the living church is essential for our growth in holiness. We have talked about holiness in our private lives and in our personal witness, but readers should not get the impression that holiness is entirely an individual and private matter. Next to life in the human Christian family, fellowship in the family of God is the best environment to learn how to grow in holiness. It is also the place where our sanctification may be tested.

We really must emphasise again that the church's health and the effectiveness of her witness depend on her obedience to the command of Jesus: 'A new command I give you: Love one another. As I have loved you, so you must love one another' (John 13:34). As we saw earlier, without this, our verbal witness becomes a lie, our worship pretence and our fellowship a sham.

We must also understand that our personal growth in holiness depends on our loving relationships with others in the fellowship of the church. It is in our interaction with each other, as well as with the worship and teaching, that we become more like Jesus.

'Ah, but' someone will say, 'what about those petty-minded Christians?' The first thing to say is that we admit that the childish behaviour of some who profess to belong to Jesus Christ is a deeply disturbing reality. It is no use trying to deny it. What these people do not, or will not realise, is that they are sinning against God, against the church and against themselves. Nor do they understand that they are erecting a barrier to the spiritual growth of others.

Looking back over my own experience, some church people – thankfully not many – stand out in my mind. I call them church people because I find it hard to call them Christian. Indeed, it is with some reluctance that I call them church people. They are determined not to forgive others for things they have said and done, some nursing petty grievances against other members of the church or against the minister for many years.

There is a lesson to be learned nevertheless. Not one of them made any progress in the Christian life. They remind me of Jude's description of the godless men who 'secretly slipped in among you' except that in this case some had been members of the church for a long time. They are certainly 'blemishes at your love feasts, eating with you without the slightest qualm' (Jude 4,12).

Make no mistake about it, an unforgiving spirit is the great enemy of joyful progress in holy living. True saints should never be guilty of it. To create disharmony in the church of Christ is a very serious thing to do and those who deliberately engage in it will, one day, be called to account.

The following words of Jesus must apply in these situations: 'For if you forgive men when they sin against you, your heavenly Father will also forgive you. But if you do not forgive men their sins, your Father will not forgive your sins' (Matt. 6:14-15). Jesus is not teaching that by forgiving others we merit our own forgiveness. He is simply laying down a condition for his disciples. How can anyone be a Christian and not forgive?

The writer to the Hebrews backs this up with a further warning: 'Make every effort to live in peace with all men and to be holy; without holiness no-one will see the Lord. See to it that no-one misses the grace of God and that no bitter root grows up to cause trouble and defile many' (Heb. 12:14-15). It is not easy to determine precisely what the writer means by missing the grace of God. He may be talking about a saint who has fallen temporarily, or about those who make a profession only to renounce it later. Either way, the bitter root will grow unless it is dealt with firmly.

We have to admit that such is our sinful nature, that even the saints can be guilty of petty-mindedness. And such are our likes and dislikes, we shall not find a church where every member is easy to get on with. Some members in the churches where I have served, I would never have chosen as friends in a thousand years. But now I do not have that choice. God does the choosing now. Indeed, how we get on with Christian people whom we would never have chosen as friends is an excellent indicator of our progress. Remember, we are not called to like them, but to love them.

In my home, we still use an old carving knife. It was a wedding present. It has been sharpened so many times, the blade is nowhere near as wide as it used to be. Sometimes, when I am sharpening it with the steel, the old proverb comes to mind: 'As iron sharpens iron, so one man sharpens another' (Proverbs 27:17).

This is what should be happening in the church fellowship all the time. As Matthew Henry comments, 'Good men's graces are sharpened by converse with those who are good' (*Exposition of the Old and New Testament*, J. Nisbet & Co.). Therefore, saints are not 'to give up meeting together, as some are in the habit of doing…' On the contrary, we are to 'consider how we may spur one another on toward love and good deeds' (Heb. 10:23-25). Absentees cannot do this.

The responsibility of builders

Almost three hundred construction workers were erecting a high building in Nairobi, Kenya. One day, after their lunch break, most were taking a nap. All of a sudden, the five-storey construction started to sway and then collapsed, killing eleven people and injuring many more. A leading politician who visited the site afterwards pointed out the importance of ensuring that only properly designed buildings are erected – a classic example of stating the obvious!

Paul too was stating the obvious when he was giving advice on how to build the church: 'But each one should be careful how he builds' (1 Cor. 3:10). The apostle pictures the church as a temple under construction and preachers (in particular) as the labourers. His advice must be taken to heart by all labourers no matter what their particular task.

Being sanctified by the truth (John 17:17) is an essential qualification for builders. We do not build a lasting structure with bickering and petty-mindedness, but with the truth. This is what Paul meant when he said: 'If any man builds on this foundation using gold, silver, costly stones, wood, hay or straw, his work will be shown for what it is, because the Day will bring it to light' (1 Cor. 3:12).

The apostle is talking about the great Day of Judgment when the fire will test every builder's work. The work of those who have built with the durable materials will stand. But those who have built with combustible materials will suffer loss because their labour has been in vain.

The words 'suffer loss' mean that shoddy builders will not receive their reward. By contrast, the believer who builds well 'will receive his reward' (1 Cor. 3:14). We are content that this has nothing to do with the gift of eternal life because even the builder whose work is poor will be saved 'but only as one escaping through the flames' Eternal life is secured for him by the fact that he has been building on the right foundation.

Even so, we must not miss the solemnity of the warning. 'Watch out that you do not lose what you have worked for, but that you may be rewarded fully' says the apostle John (2 John 8). Clearly, there is a reward for faithful service and every believer should strive for it. Now, not later, is the time to start.

It is important to emphasise that we are talking here about rewards for faithful service and not about being eternally lost. We shall come back to this subject in chapter 22, where we shall point out the vital difference between losing the reward and losing salvation altogether.

The glory of togetherness

The togetherness of the saints in this life will be more than preserved when Christ returns. On that day we shall all be glorified together. 'The dead in Christ will rise first' and then 'we who are still alive and are left will be caught up together with them...' More than that, we shall be together 'with the Lord for ever' (1 Thess. 4:16-18).

This glorious fact calls for some heart-searching. What is my contribution to that glorious togetherness? Am I guilty of anything that would hinder progress or discourage my fellow builders? Am I a faithful builder? Do I pull my weight or do the other builders have to work overtime because I am 'on strike' for most of the time? Why should I suffer loss at the Day of Judgment? Why should I scrape into heaven 'as one escaping through the flames' (1 Cor. 3:15)? Why should all my labour count for nothing?

12. God's covenant

The saints' security

Covenant theology! Some believers fight shy of these two words. They regard the subject as either something approved of by people who are extreme or unorthodox, or they feel that it is an aspect of the gospel that is beyond their understanding and best left to high-powered theologians. I know my own reaction when titles like 'mathematical physics' or 'quantum mechanics' are mentioned! My guess is that this is how some feel about Covenant Theology.

This is a pity. Every saint should have a firm grasp of the subject. Not, I hasten to add, just for sake of head knowledge but for the blessings it brings. If we are to understand how sanctification fits into God's eternal plan of redemption, for example, it is essential at the very least, that we appreciate the basic principles of the Covenant of Grace.

Several covenants are revealed in the Bible. First, we have the covenant God established with Adam, then Noah. After this, God entered into a covenant with Abraham, which was renewed with his posterity, including King David of Israel. The covenant with Moses did not replace the Covenant of Grace but was introduced for reasons we shall look at shortly. Finally, came the new covenant, which we call the New Testament, and which reveals the final development of the Covenant of Grace.

Although human covenants are set up with the agreement of two parties, like marriage, God imposes his covenants without consultation with any human being. He establishes them with the people whom he chooses and we are glad that it is so. These privileged people are required to keep the covenant by obeying its terms. The Covenant of Grace, of which we shall say more shortly, is not an exception to this rule: 'Know therefore that the LORD your God is God; he is the faithful God, keeping his covenant of love to a thousand generations of those who love him and keep his commands' (Deut. 7:9).

Adam and Noah

Readers who are new to the subject, will find it helpful to consider God's covenants with Adam and Noah separately. In the narrative of God's dealings with Adam the word 'covenant' is not even mentioned. The only use of the word in this connection is to be found in Hosea 6:7. The promised blessings for obedience and the curse threatened for disobedience prove that it was a covenant.

The covenant with Adam is usually called 'The Covenant of Works' because the enjoyment of its blessings depended entirely on his obedience to the divine command. Adam failed and, as a result, sin came into the world. In theory, the principle that eternal life may be earned by perfect obedience to all God's commandments still stands. 'Moses describes in this way the righteousness that is by the law: "The man who does these things will live by them"' (Rom. 10:5). If Adam had been able to keep God's commands perfectly – or anyone else for that matter – he would have received eternal life in his own right.

Sadly, the entire human race is affected by Adam's sin. We have all inherited a sinful nature and have followed his bad example. Paul makes this clear in Romans 5:12: 'Therefore, just as sin entered the world through one man, and death through sin, and in this way death came to all men, because all sinned…'. The apostle does not complete his sentence, but what he has said is clear. The way to heaven by means of perfect obedience is closed forever because no one has the ability to achieve it.

The covenant God established with Noah (Gen. 6:18), contrasts sharply with the covenant made with Adam, because Noah did not fail. In this covenant, the Lord brought judgment on the earth because of man's wickedness. 'So the LORD said, "I will wipe mankind, whom I have created, from the face of the earth – men and animals, and creatures that move along the ground, and birds of the air…"' (Gen. 6:7). The promised blessings were to be enjoyed by the future generations.

That Noah should follow God's instructions carefully in building the ark was the only condition (Gen. 6:22). Noah was chosen because he 'was a righteous man, blameless among the people of his time, and he walked with God' (Gen. 6:9). Noah and his family, eight persons altogether, were saved.

The Covenant of Grace

The title given to this covenant, which is everlasting, rules out any suggestion that God's favour may be gained by what we do. That is to say, it does not demand perfect obedience from us in order to be saved. On the contrary, salvation is God's free gift to all who repent and believe the gospel.

The covenant really originated back in eternity when the three Person of the Trinity entered into an agreement. God the Father promised to give to his Son a people for his own possession. For his part, the Son would become a man under the law, which he would keep perfectly in order to redeem his people. The Holy Spirit would empower Christ in his great mission and apply the benefits of his death to all whom God has chosen. Many theologians regard this as a separate covenant and call it 'The Covenant of Redemption'.

As the Scripture explains, the blood of Christ sealed or ratified the Covenant of Grace, and his resurrection proves that he was qualified to do this. The writer to the Hebrews removes any doubt: 'May the God of peace, who through the blood of the eternal covenant brought back from the dead our Lord Jesus, that great Shepherd of the sheep, equip you with everything good for doing his will, and may he work in us what is pleasing to him, through Jesus Christ, to whom be glory for ever and ever. Amen' (Heb. 13:20-21).

We now begin to see how and why a clear understanding of the Covenant of Grace will give the believer an insight into God's will for his saints since before time. Of first importance, we learn that the command to be holy dominates. We also learn that God's promise that he will be our God and we his people is enshrined in the covenant.

This promise was given to Abraham back in Genesis 17:7-8 and reaches its final fulfilment in Revelation 21:3: 'And I heard a loud voice from the throne saying, "Now the dwelling of God is with men, and he will live with them. They will be his people and God himself will be with them and be their God.' The promise is repeated all through the Scriptures (Exod. 29:45; Jer. 24:7; 31:33; 2 Cor. 6:18). Apart from this promise, there is no holiness and no heaven for anyone.

At least three serious errors about the Covenant of Grace are in circulation. First, some Christians think of the entire Old Testament as the 'Law'. They wrongly suppose that the only covenant in the Old Testament is the covenant with Moses. For them, grace is confined to the New Testament and is seen as a new beginning. In part, this may be because the Letter to the Hebrews refers to the covenant with Moses as the 'first covenant' (Heb. 9:1) and it is so easy to think he is referring to everything between Genesis and Malachi.

As a result, these believers do not think of the Covenant of Grace as something God planned back in eternity. Nor do they realise the significance of God's covenant with Abraham. If they did, they would know that they are the true children of Abraham because God told him, 'Listen to whatever Sarah tells you, because it is through Isaac that your offspring will be reckoned' (Gen. 21:12).

Paul takes up the theme and explains that Christian believers, Jew or Gentile, are God's children. Natural descent from Abraham counts for nothing: '"It is through Isaac that your offspring will be reckoned." In other words, it is not the natural children who are God's children, but it is the children of the promise who are regarded as Abraham's offspring' (Rom. 9:7-8).

As Paul explains, the covenant with Moses came after the Covenant of Grace was established with Abraham: 'The promises were spoken to Abraham and to his seed… The law, introduced 430 years later, does not set aside the covenant previously established by God and thus do away with the promise' (Gal. 3:16,17). The Covenant of Grace continues forever and overarches the Mosaic Covenant.

God did not change his mind about the Covenant of Grace. The New Testament is not plan B, but the outworking of the covenant. 'God is not a man, that he should lie, nor a son of man, that he should change his mind. Does he speak and then not act? Does he promise and not fulfil?' (Num. 23:19).

The New Testament (or Covenant) brings a fuller revelation of the content of the Covenant of Grace, but it is, nevertheless, a development of God's eternal plan of redemption and not a new beginning. The covenant established with Abraham is never referred to as 'Old' anywhere in Scripture. The various covenants are developments in God's eternal plan and there is a unity and continuity in them.

Second, the idea is abroad that God has lowered his standards in the New Covenant. The demand for holiness, it is thought, is not as important under grace as it was under the law. This is a most serious error. The level of obedience God requires is the same in

the New Testament as it was in the Old. The beneficiaries of the
New Covenant are to make every effort to be holy, for 'without
holiness, no-one will see the Lord' (Heb. 12:14). It is also true to
say that without holiness, no-one can enjoy fellowship with the
Lord.

'Ah, but' some will say, 'under the terms of the Covenant
with Moses, the standard required was perfect obedience to
God's commandments and no one can reach that standard. This
means that God has indeed lowered his standard.' Not at all! It
has already been pointed out that those who want to be justified
by the law must live perfect lives, and, as James says, 'Whoever
stumbles at just one point is guilty of breaking all of it' (James
2:10). Nevertheless, as we saw in chapter eight, God's standard
never changes. If God could lower his standard under the New
Covenant, then why did he not do it under the Old one established
with Moses? If it were possible for God to lower his standards,
Christ's death would not have been necessary.

Christ fulfilled that high standard on our behalf. This is why his
sacrifice is acceptable to the Father as the price of our redemption.
In view of this amazing grace, anyone who thinks God is not now so
severe is deceiving himself. To think that because Christ forgives,
we can continue in sin is to play fast and loose with divine grace.
Those who do it will perish.

Obviously, as the writer to the Hebrews points out, the New
Covenant (the Covenant of Grace) is a better covenant than the
covenant with Moses. 'For if there had been nothing wrong with
that first covenant, [the covenant with Moses] no place would
have been sought for another…' (Heb. 8:7). It is better, not least
because it is a covenant of the Spirit. Again, let Paul explain: 'He
[God] has made us competent as ministers of a new covenant – not
of the letter but of the Spirit; for the letter kills, but the Spirit gives
life' (2 Cor. 3:6).

Nevertheless, as we have just seen, the covenant with Moses
was a necessary development of the Covenant of Grace. It was

designed to point to the only One through whom redemption is realised. As Paul puts it, 'the law was put in charge to lead us to Christ that we might be justified by faith' (Gal. 3:24).

The terms of the covenant with Moses should be familiar to us. The Ten Commandments have not been consigned to history as is often thought. Indeed, they still stand as the covenant lifestyle. This is how God expects his saints to behave. For this reason alone, the covenant with Moses was not a new beginning. It was a logical continuation of the covenant with Abraham. The same applies to the covenant with David and the New Covenant itself.

In the New Covenant Jeremiah's prophecy is fulfilled: '"This is the covenant I will make with the house of Israel after that time," declares the LORD. "I will put my law in their minds and write it on their hearts. I will be their God and they will be my people"' (Jer. 31:33). Clearly, having God's law written on our hearts will give the saints more awareness of God's demand for obedience and not less.

The third mistake is to conclude that the blessings of forgiveness and justification were not available in Old Testament times. If this were the case, how were sinful men like Noah, Abraham, Isaac, Jacob, Moses, David and many more, justified by faith? True, they did not have the blessing of 'another Counsellor to be with you forever – the Spirit of truth' (John 14:16-17). Nevertheless, all God's people, no matter when they live or have lived, inherit the benefits of Christ's sacrifice.

Why then, did the faithful men and women in the Old Testament not receive all the blessings of the Covenant? The writer to the Hebrews tells us that the greatest blessings are yet future, which means that we who are alive have not yet received them. The saints in the Old Testament 'did not receive the things promised; they only saw them and welcomed them from a distance… God had planned something better for us so that only together with us would they be made perfect' (Heb. 11:13,40). We are back to that togetherness we spoke about earlier. When God's covenant promise to be with us and to be our God reaches its final fulfilment, we shall all be glorified together. There will be no private glorifications!

The two comings of Christ then, are the crowning glory of the Covenant of Grace. Jeremiah the prophet gives us a very interesting insight into the nature of his first coming: '"The days are coming," declares the LORD, "when I will fulfil the gracious promise I made to the house of Israel and to the house of Judah. In those days and at that time I will make a righteous Branch sprout from David's line"' (Jer. 33:14-15). Christ is that righteous branch.

The prophet continues: 'This is what the LORD says: "If you can break my covenant with the day and my covenant with the night, so that day and night no longer come at their appointed time, then my covenant with David my servant... can be broken, and David will no longer have a descendent to reign on his throne"' (Jer. 33:20-21). This is nothing short of a divine undertaking to ensure that great David's greater Son will reign forever under the terms of the Covenant of Grace.

How exciting! As sure as the sun will set this evening and rise again tomorrow morning, so certain is our position as the redeemed children of God. For we are 'heirs of God and co-heirs with Christ, if indeed we share in his sufferings in order that we may also share in his glory' (Rom. 8:17). God will never cast us off. We have a High Priest who sacrificed himself for the transgressions of all his people. He is the mediator of the Covenant, 'that those who are called may receive the promised eternal inheritance – now that he has died as a ransom to set them free from the sins committed under the first covenant' (Heb 9:15). What an incentive to holy living!

A lot more could be said on this subject, but the main thing we need to remember is that God is working his purpose out and we, the true sons of Abraham, are called to be 'a holy nation' (1 Peter 2:9). To this we briefly turn.

Holiness is central

There can be no doubt that holiness of life is the most important
expression of the covenant relationship. How can it be otherwise
when we are in fellowship with a holy God? The call to holiness
has always been central as both Testaments testify: 'I am the LORD
your God; consecrate yourselves and be holy, because I am holy'
(Lev. 11:44). 'For God did not call us to be impure but to live a
holy life' (1 Thess. 4:7).

As we saw earlier, election and holiness belong together. We
are called to be holy (1 Peter 1:15). We are 'predestined to be
conformed to the likeness of his Son' (Rom. 8:29). We are 'called
to be saints' (Rom. 1:7). Our Saviour Jesus Christ 'gave himself
for us to redeem us from all wickedness and to purify for himself
a people that are his very own, eager to do what is good' (Titus
2:14). God chose us in Christ 'before the creation of the world, to
be holy and blameless in his sight' (Eph 1:4).

13. God's guidance

The saints' vocation

'I feel led'

Most of my fellow-students in college were keenly aware of the possibility of self-deception in the matter of guidance. The three words 'I feel led' when used by the students were always greeted with sceptical laughter. Young men, especially where the opposite sex is concerned, can easily persuade themselves that this or that course of action is God's will for them.

In later years, when the claim 'God has told me' came into common use, 'I feel led' no longer seemed so extreme. At least there was then a tacit admission that human feeling had something to do with the guidance being claimed. Now, we are faced with claims to direct revelation. This is harder to deal with. In many such cases in my own experience, God was blamed for actions that were obviously wrong or even immoral, like the Christian woman who told me that God had told her to go and live with someone else's husband!

Some claim Biblical support for this method of guidance because there are many instances in Scripture when God spoke directly to his servants. One example will suffice: 'Now an angel of the Lord said to Philip, "Go south to the road – the desert road – that goes down from Jerusalem to Gaza"' (Acts 8:26). Philip obeyed and found himself talking to the Ethiopian eunuch, an important official in the Ethiopian government.

Why, then, you may ask, is it no longer legitimate to seek guidance like this? The proper question is, does God still give guidance like this? In view of God's promise of wisdom and the guidance he gives in Scripture, do we really need to hear voices? Where does God's Word promise that he will now by-pass our enlightened understanding and give us direct revelations?

Our safe guide

Turning to the Scriptures, we are confronted with many promises that God will guide his people into the right way. Proverbs 3:5-6, for example, is printed indelibly on my heart because the donor of one of my Bibles, long since worn out, had written it on the front flyleaf: 'Trust in the LORD with all your heart and lean not on your own understanding; in all your ways acknowledge him, and he will make your paths straight.'

There are many more such promises: 'I will instruct and teach you in the way you should go; I will counsel you and watch over you' (Ps. 32:8). 'Who, then, is the man that fears the LORD? He will instruct him in the way chosen for him' (Ps. 25:12). The heart-warming aspect of these promises is that God takes us along with him so that we do not always know where we are heading. We become party to his will for us.

Consecration, commitment and consultation

The apostle urges us to offer our bodies as living sacrifices to God, which is our spiritual worship: 'Do not conform any longer to the pattern of this world, but be transformed by the renewing of your mind. Then you will be able to test and approve what God's will is – his good, pleasing and perfect will' (Rom. 12:1-2). Paul is saying that knowing God's will is the result of our consecration to God. By this means, we develop the ability to discern what is and what is not pleasing to God.

Scripture guides us in two ways. It gives clear but general instructions on how saints are to live in this world. God's will as far as our behaviour is concerned is the same for all. It also lays down principles by which we are to judge whether our proposed plans are right or wrong. These principles are also the same for all, but the matter under consideration will be different in each case.

God's guidance for our daily behaviour must come first. It is no use trying to find God's will on matters like choosing a wife, or a job, or a place to live, if we are not interested in practical daily holiness. If our lives are not consecrated to God, we cannot expect him to guide us in the perplexing situations life brings.

Two things we should always remember. First, whatever way we decide to take, it must be the way of holiness. If our contemplated course of action involves anything that is contrary to the will of God for his saints, it is obviously wrong. Second, after we have made a decision, we must be committed to it, unless of course, it is clearly flawed. We do ourselves no favours if we keep changing our minds. If it turns out that we were not in possession of all the relevant facts when the decision was made, it does not necessarily mean that we have made a mistake.

For example, Tom, after due consultation and prayer, decides that Mary is the woman he should marry. Mary agrees. Then, after the wedding, they both discover that their partner has blemishes of character that they were not aware of. Mary is not the angel Tom thought, and Tom has a selfish streak in his character that Mary had not seen. They cannot then decide to separate on the assumption that it was not God's will after all.

Thinking Biblically about things like choosing a wife, or a job, or a place to live is a demanding discipline. This is why, especially for younger believers, it is vital to consult older and more mature believers, in confidence. In fact, this is one of the Biblical principles I am talking about. 'The way of a fool seems right to him, but a wise man listens to advice' (Prov. 12:15).

14. God's enabling

The saints' resources

The process of producing a beautiful diamond is an excellent illustration of the Holy Spirit's work in the life of the believer. Without the skilled working of the divine Lapidary, the redeemed sinner's potential to radiate the beauty of Christ could never be realised. As it is, God takes him just as he is in all his filth and, with his co-operation, begins the life-long process of knocking off the rough corners and wearing away the unwanted material on the wheel of life. The Spirit's aim is to gradually make the sinner more efficient in reflecting the glory of Jesus so that he moves forward towards perfection. We shall come back to this later in the chapter.

The Trinity at work

When one Person of the Trinity is assigned to a particular task, the other two Persons are always involved. It would be correct to say that sanctification is the work of our Triune God. Although it is predominantly the work of the Holy Spirit, both God the Father and God the Son each have a part to play. Our high calling to holiness would not exist if the Father had not chosen us. The process could not begin without the redemption purchased for us by the death of the Son. And where would we be without his teaching and example?

The apostle Peter provides us with a superb summary of the role of the Trinity in the work of sanctification: '...we have been chosen according to the foreknowledge of God the Father, through the sanctifying work of the Holy Spirit, for obedience to Jesus Christ...' (1 Peter 1:2).

From this one verse, we learn four vital truths. First, all three Persons work together to call and prepare sinners for the glory to come. Second, the Father chooses those who are to be prepared in this way. Third, the Spirit does the work of calling them and making them saintly in character. Fourth, obedience to Christ is the end in view, for to be saintly consists in obeying him.

Although the Spirit, in his grace, delights to co-operate with us, our ability to co-operate with him is implanted in us by the same Spirit. There is nothing in our sinful nature that would move one inch towards such co-operation. Standards of morality established by the power of the will have nothing to do with holiness. Those who have doubts on this point should examine more carefully the weight of evidence in the Scriptures.

The areas in which we are enabled to co-operate with the Spirit are to be found mainly in our use of the means of grace. Take, for example, worship, fellowship and teaching. These are God's gifts to us and we are responsible for our use of them. True, the Holy Spirit is the One who warms our hearts as the Scriptures are opened to us (Luke 24:32) and he is the author of the joy we have in worship and fellowship. But we benefit from neither if we are absent when the church meets.

Appreciation of the God-given privilege of co-operating with the Spirit in the use and development of all these precious gifts is wearing thin in today's church. For example, there are mature Christians in the church who are willing to advise us but are seldom consulted. They too are God's gifts to us. I am deeply indebted to many such men and women (including my wife) whose advice saved me from many pitfalls. I did nothing to deserve it. But there was a lot I could do to derive the maximum benefit from it.

Whenever we fail, through our own fault, to use the means of grace to the full, we not only inflict injury on ourselves but also on the church. Many problems that trouble the saints would be solved if they did not absent themselves from the church's worship, prayer and teaching sessions.

The Spirit's work is thorough

The Spirit of God is always at work in every area of the believer's life. He is increasingly disposing the saint's will, his mind and emotions towards pleasing God. This is in line with the Old Testament covenant promise: 'I will put my law in their minds and write it on their hearts' (Jer. 31:33). In order to please God we must be obedient to his Word, and to be obedient, we must know it. We looked at this in chapter 9.

Later on, we shall also look in a little more detail at the reasons why, in spite of our efforts, we are unable to reach the level of perfect obedience. But we rejoice in the fact that, in the new birth, God has radically changed our attitudes so that we are now able to love God. This again is in line with the covenant promise of the Old Testament 'I will give you a new heart and put a new spirit in you; I will remove from you your heart of stone and give you a heart of flesh. And I will put my Spirit in you and move you to follow my decrees and be careful to keep my laws' (Ezek. 36:26-27).

It is well worth taking time to ponder these marvellous promises. Take, for example, what the apostle Peter says about them. God 'has given us his very great and precious promises, so that through them you may participate in the divine nature...' (2 Peter 1:4). We cannot possibly get our heads round this. Nevertheless, we experience sheer joy that such promises are fulfilled in us. It is quite breathtaking!

I love Calvin's comment: 'If our Lord will share his glory, power, and righteousness with the elect, nay, will give himself to be enjoyed by them; and what is better still, will, in a manner, become one with them, let us remember that every kind of happiness is herein included. And when we have made great progress in thus meditating, let us understand that if the conceptions of our minds are contrasted with the sublimity of the mystery, we are still halting at the very entrance' (*Institutes of the Christian Religion*, Eerdmans Publishing Co. Book III, Ch 25, page 273).

Even though we understand but a small fraction of the mystery in this life, this kind of meditation helps us to assess how far we have come and what glory and happiness remains to be explored and experienced before we depart this life. It also helps us to see why being born of the Spirit must lead to the renewal of God's likeness in us (Eph. 4:24). Since Christ is in us (Col. 1:27), and we in him, every part of our lives is bound to change, for 'if anyone is in Christ, he is a new creation; the old has passed away, the new has come!' (2 Cor. 5:17). As Jesus said, 'Make the tree good and its fruit will be good' (Matt. 12:33).

The old jibe that saints can be so heavenly-minded that they are of no earthly use is a mischievous lie. The more heavenly-minded we are, the more earthly use we shall be. In other words, the more we fix our eyes on Jesus, the more God will use us for his glory in this world. It is possible of course, for a believer to live with his head in the clouds but this has nothing whatever to do with heavenly-mindedness.

Scripture makes it abundantly clear that when we see the Lord Jesus Christ in all his glory, we shall be transformed into his likeness in an instant. For 'we know that when he appears, we shall be like him, for we shall see him as he is' (1 John 3:2). Seeing him will be the cause, and being changed into his likeness will be the effect.

But what we easily overlook is that this principle is in operation right now. Seeing Jesus by faith is the cause, and being changed gradually into his likeness is the effect. The secret of growth here and now, therefore, is to keep our eyes on Jesus because the holiness to which we aspire is supremely revealed in him. I am persuaded that believers who make a habit of fixing their eyes on Jesus (Heb. 12:2) will never stop longing for more.

Paul takes this principle for granted: 'And we, who with unveiled faces all reflect the Lord's glory, are being transformed into his likeness with ever-increasing glory, which comes from the Lord, who is the Spirit' (2 Cor. 3:18). I prefer the New King James Version: 'But we all, with unveiled face, beholding as in a mirror the glory of the Lord, are being transformed into the same image from glory to glory...' The apostle has just been talking about Moses, whose face, when he came down the mountain after receiving the commandments, was so radiant that Aaron and all the Israelites were afraid to come near him. So Moses put a veil over his face (Exod. 34:29-35). Now Paul draws an important lesson from this. He makes the point in 2 Cor. 3:14 that the glory of God is still veiled to the Israelites, but 'whenever anyone turns to the Lord, the veil is taken away.'

We know that even for those for whom the veil has been removed see 'but a poor reflection' (1 Cor. 13:12). Usually, a mirror is used to show us what our faces are like, but in this case, we are not looking at ourselves but Jesus. In Paul's time, mirrors were not made from the high quality glass we use today. Even so, the image of Christ we now see by faith is imperfect, which means that our present sanctification will also be imperfect.

But we also know that although our vision of Christ is imperfect, he is not hidden. The sight of him is life changing and character forming and we should not underestimate its power. As our view of his glory, as it is revealed in the Scriptures, grows brighter, the desire to be like him is bound to grow stronger.

Like the Israelites, when we were slaves to sin, we too were unable to see Jesus because 'the man without the Spirit does not accept the things that come from the Spirit of God, for they are foolishness to him and he cannot understand them…' (1 Cor. 2:14). But now the veil has been removed so that we can understand the Scriptures (Luke 24:45) it means we do not have much time left in which to 'throw off the sin that hinders and the sin that so easily entangles,' so that we may 'run with perseverance the race marked out for us' (Heb. 12:1).

The Spirit's work is powerful

Television advertisements for products to help people stop smoking usually stop short of claiming success without the co-operation of the patient. This nicotine patch will help you, the makers say, but the rest is left to your will-power. Will-power in this case, has to do with the ability to resist the craving to smoke.

In its broader sense, strong will-power means having the strength of will to carry out our decisions and plans. Some would go as far as to claim that will-power can determine a person's destiny. If, by the word 'destiny' the claimants mean eternal destiny, we take leave to disagree. Men may have physical strength, intellectual strength and emotional strength which will assist them in the limited business of making headway in their field, but when it comes to determining our eternal destiny, human will-power is powerless.

'You see' says Paul, 'at just the right time, when we were still powerless, Christ died for the ungodly' (Rom. 5:6). There can be no doubt about the apostle's meaning. We were destitute of spiritual strength to help ourselves. We were drawn to Christ by the Father (John 6:44). His was the power that brought the serious nature of our sins to light. We were, and still are, utterly dependent on him for the gift of repentance and faith. And, but for the power of God the Holy Spirit within us, we would be just as helpless to obey God's call to holiness.

Forming good habits by the power of the will is no bad thing, but we do not become saintly in character by our own will-power, but by the power of Christ in us. Without him, our interest in holy living would wither and die. We would be unable to maintain any interest in holiness whatsoever.

How thankful then we need to be that the Holy Spirit is with us for ever. Although we are commanded to be holy, which means co-operating with the Spirit in the strength he gives, there are times when we may feel as though he has departed from us. Feelings however, are not a safe indicator of divine activity. If we keep short accounts with God, not allowing sin to go unconfessed, the new life of the Spirit will sustain us throughout our pilgrimage, no matter how we feel.

If confirmation of this truth were needed, Peter provides it: 'His divine power has given us everything we need for life and godliness through our knowledge of him who called us by his own glory and goodness. Through these he has given us his very great and precious promises, so that through them you may participate in the divine nature and escape the corruption in the world caused by evil desires' (2 Peter 1:3-4).

All too often, it is assumed that the Holy Spirit gives power to the saints so that it becomes their own possession to use as they see fit. The ongoing interest in the church in having miraculous powers (1 Cor. 12:10) obscures the need to recognise that God's power 'is made perfect in weakness'. The apostle Paul says, 'I will boast ... about my weaknesses, so that Christ's power may rest on me' (2 Cor. 12:9).

Painting is one of my hobbies. If I want some feature in my painting to stand out, I need to make sure that the surrounding area is painted in a contrasting colour or shade. If, say, the feature were white, it would not be seen if the background were also white. We all know how difficult it is to read black print on darkly coloured paper. So it is with God's power. The greater our weakness, the more conspicuous his power becomes. This is why Paul boasted in his weakness.

Paul, of course, was talking about his 'thorn in the flesh', which was almost certainly a physical malady of some sort. But the same is true in the matter of sanctification. If we really want to grow in holiness, the first thing we have to do is to recognise our own weakness. To work on the principle that we ourselves have the power to become more like Jesus, always leads to a divine power-cut!

Diamonds

When a diamond is mined, it is most unattractive. Faced with the shape of the mined stone, the diamond cutter decides what size and shape of diamond is best because every stone is different. First, the rubbish has to be removed and then cutting and polishing has to be done before the beauty of the finished diamond is revealed. This is slow and highly skilled work. During the process a considerable weight loss occurs, perhaps even to half of the original weight of the mined stone. Where possible, everything that would spoil the beauty of the diamond must be removed.

The 'brilliant' cut is now regarded as the best shape to provide maximum brilliance. It consists of fifty-eight facets, each carefully polished to its exact shape and size on the lapidary's wheel. There are thirty-three such facets on the crown, and twenty-five below, on what is called the pavilion. The beauty of the diamond is made up of both reflections of light and what is called 'fire' – the flashes of the colours of the spectrum as the diamond is moved.

As the work proceeds, the material removed gets smaller and the polishing finer. Similarly, when believers reach maturity we would expect them to be past the stage where rough cutting has to be used. If, after many years of discipleship a believer does not reflect a little of the glory of Jesus, something has gone seriously wrong.

As we saw at the beginning of the chapter, God is the divine lapidary. He uses the ups and downs of life as his tools to shape the saint so that he reflects more and more of the glory of Christ. There will be times when the process is painful. We need always to remember that the ultimate good towards which all things work for the believer (Rom. 8:28) is not a trouble-free life, but conformity to Christ (verse 29).

Strange as it may seem to those with no experience of the help of the Spirit, this gradual process will not make the saint feel good about himself. On the contrary, blemishes of character will continue to be revealed, some of which he was formerly unaware. Indeed, such is the depth of depravity of the sinful nature, this will be the case right to the end of his life on earth.

In addition, as he grows in holiness, sin will become more serious to him. The fact that he will hate his sins more and more will ensure that he will be more conscious of them at the end of his journey than he was at the beginning. For this reason, he will never boast of his attainments. As the years go by, the tax-collector's words – 'God have mercy on me, a sinner' (Luke 18:13), will come even more readily to his lips.

Before we became Christians, we were 'dead in trespasses and sins' (Eph 2:1), but 'God, who is rich in mercy, made us alive with Christ' (Eph 2:4-5). Now, in the strength God gives, we are enabled to co-operate with him in our growth in holiness – something we could never do before.

Part Three

The saints' progress

15. Undivided loyalty

What is the saints' responsibility?

A single purpose

I have to attend the eye clinic at the local hospital once a year to make sure that my diabetes is not affecting my eyes. Sometimes, they put drops in my eyes before taking a photograph. When this happens, they warn me not to drive for two hours because my vision is blurred. When the traffic lights are showing red, for instance, I see two red lights, one above the other. It is a timely reminder of how precious my sight is to me and how much I depend upon it.

It also gives some insight into the meaning of the words of Jesus: 'The eye is the lamp of the body. If your eyes are good, your whole body will be full of light. But if your eyes are bad, your whole body will be full of darkness' (Matt. 6:22-23). When I was young in the faith, I could not make any sense of this verse. In what way, I wondered, can the eye be the light of the body? Has it to do with inner enlightenment, light entering the body to furnish the brain with information, or was Jesus talking about the necessity for clear sight if we are to find our way around without walking into a lamppost?

Today, it makes a lot more sense to me. The older versions of the Bible translate it: 'If therefore thine eye be single...' The word 'single', which has arguments in its favour as an acceptable translation, gives us the clue to the Lord's meaning. He is talking about the need for undivided loyalty to God. If we have double vision, we are likely to stumble because the brain cannot interpret the image properly. In the same way, a divided loyalty will lead to a fall.

James Allen (1864-1912), an English philosophical writer, said some strange things. One of his statements however, gives good advice: 'Above all be of single aim; have a legitimate and useful purpose, and devote yourself unreservedly to it.' Of course, it would have been even better if Mr Allen had been able to say what the aim should be.

Jesus himself is our finest example in this matter. He devoted himself unreservedly to the will of his Father. We read that as the time approached for him to be taken up to heaven, he 'resolutely set out for Jerusalem' (Luke 9:51). Knowing what suffering awaited him in the city, he did not hesitate or procrastinate. It was his Father's will that he should die for the sins of the world.

Familiarity with the story can easily blind us to the intensity of his suffering. At least we should know by now why he did it. He went to Jerusalem to reconcile God's people to himself, for 'when we were God's enemies, we were reconciled to him through the death of his Son' (Rom. 5:10). He went to the cross to satisfy the just demands of a holy God on our behalf: 'Since we have now been justified by his blood, how much more shall we be saved from God's wrath through him!' (Rom. 5:9).

His accomplishment does not make sense unless we understand that it was to redeem his people and make them holy. As the old hymn puts it, 'He died to make us good.' And, as Paul puts it, he 'gave himself for us to redeem us from all wickedness and to purify a people that are his very own, eager to do what is good' (Titus 2:14). He also faced the agony resolutely so that we, his saints, have his example of self-sacrifice. The world affords no better example of a man with a single purpose.

In passing, we should take note that a true saint cannot be redeemed but not purified, or purified but not redeemed. The two belong together. We are redeemed in order to be purified – people who are characterised by doing what is good. There are to be no dark corners or inaccessible rooms in our lives. The entire house must be 'swept clean and put in order' (Matt. 12:44) so that our new owner may live in it. We are not to hide the clutter in the attic and then lock the door, but get rid of it altogether. Indeed, if there are 'no-go' areas in our lives, this is the best place to start.

A fellow minister phoned me to say that a believer, a prominent and useful member of his church, had left his wife for another woman and that he was now living in my area. The following Sunday morning I observed a stranger coming into the church with a Bible under his arm. The person on duty at the door warmly greeted the man and after the service, several people did the same.

I managed to find out where the man was living and during the following week, I called at the house. Both he and his illicit partner were in. During the rather awkward conversation, he told me that he wanted to get in and out of the church without speaking to anyone, but it seemed as if everyone wanted to talk with him! The woman was obviously not a believer. As graciously as I could, I pointed out that what they were doing was wrong and I left.

It was perfectly clear to me during my visit that the man was now intending to carry on with his outwardly Christian way of life as before, and enjoy his relationship with this other woman. He should have known it was not possible. That he should be attempting to do this after being a Christian for such a long time was, for me, a warning never to underestimate the ability of the sinful nature to justify its own actions. It was also clear to me that the Lord had no intention of leaving his sinning child in peace.

When Paul said: 'It is God's will that you should be sanctified' he was talking about sexual morality and the need to learn how to control our bodies (1 Thess. 4:3-8). The alternative reading at verse four says: 'that each of you should learn to live with his own wife' or 'learn how to acquire a wife.' This is an area where we are vulnerable at any age.

Many years ago, some older missionaries visited the church where I was the minister. During a meeting at the vicarage, we were discussing the temptations to which missionaries are exposed. A man who had served for many years in East Africa said something that has remained with me ever since: 'When I was young and virile, I assumed that in my old age Satan would no longer tempt me sexually. I was wrong. He never gives up.'

Of course, Paul did not confine holiness to sexual purity. No part of our lives is excluded from God's requirement. Later, in the same letter the apostle writes: 'May God himself, the God of peace, sanctify you through and through. May your whole spirit, soul and body be kept blameless at the coming of our Lord Jesus Christ' (1 Thess. 5:23). There are no exceptions.

Naaman, the commander-in-chief of the army of the king of Aram, was another example of a man who was not single-minded. He was a leper, and being a man of high rank, he was too proud to go and dip himself seven times in the river Jordan as the prophet Elisha had directed him. Why could he not wash in the rivers of Damascus and be cleansed from his leprosy? Were they not far better than the river Jordan?

The commander's servants had more sense than their master. They persuaded him to do as he was told. So Naaman dipped himself seven times in the Jordan 'and his flesh was restored like that of a young boy' (2 Kings 5:14). The officer was very thankful and vowed never again to offer sacrifices to any other god but the LORD.

Then, a little 'but' entered his vow: 'But may the LORD forgive your servant for this one thing: when my master enters the temple of Rimmon to bow down and he is leaning on my arm and I bow down there also – when I bow down in the temple of Rimmon, may the LORD forgive your servant for this' (2 Kings 5:18).

Now Rimmon was a false god whose temple was also situated in Damascus. Evidently, both the king of Aram and Naaman his commander were regular worshippers. Naaman was now trying to reserve the right to continue to bow down to a false god in the hope that God would forgive him. Apparently, the cost of refusing to do so was too great for him. (2 Kings 5:1-19 tells the whole story.)

Where holiness is concerned, such double-mindedness is out of the question. Every saint is called to be holy in every part of his being – body, will, mind and heart. He is also called to be holy in every department of his life – home, work, church and his private life. As soon as we begin to try to hide something, we grieve the Holy Spirit.

Beware hypocrisy

A reliable friend told me that his uncle, an elder in a closed Brethren Assembly, kept his television set behind a curtain in a private room. It was out of bounds to everyone except himself and his wife. Along with his fellow elders, he had issued an edict to the members of the church that they were not to watch television because it was of the devil. When people called to see him, he welcomed them heartily, but made sure they were entertained in a different room.

Living a lie like this is even worse than double-mindedness. It is hypocrisy of the worst kind – the very sin that made Jesus angry. Saints should avoid it like the plague. But let us not pretend that we could never be guilty of it. I know from experience how easy it is to have that curtained corner; how easy it is to put on a good face when it matters. Indeed, it is not all that difficult to convince ourselves that we can keep God in ignorance!

The sinful mind is capable of adopting the most inexcusable self-deception in order to justify hypocritical behaviour. What's more, it can keep it up for a long time. While we tolerate and continue in sin, we cannot grow in holiness. We need to pray constantly that God will guard us from sin.

I am inclined to think that King David's adultery with Bathsheba, appalling though it was, is no worse than the above example of hypocrisy. It is, however, a vivid warning to all God's saints. It all began in David's heart when, idling on the palace roof, he saw Bathsheba bathing (2 Sam. 11:2). All his efforts to cover up his sin were thwarted. God was displeased, but remained faithful to his child by sending Nathan the prophet to expose the king's horrid transgression. This is why, after his repentance, he said to the Lord, 'Surely you desire truth in the inner parts ... Create in me a pure heart, O God' (Ps. 51:6,10).

The other day I read an article about the development of mobile phones. The author was giving his reasons why he preferred the single-purpose devices rather than the phones that incorporate cameras, ipods and digital audio players. He rounded off the article by saying that dedicated single-purpose devices will remain the best way for people to satisfy their highly technical needs.

It occurred to me that if the saints are to satisfy their highly spiritual needs, they too have to be single-purpose people. The trouble is that our old sinful nature will always try to halt or slow down the purpose for which we were redeemed and put a check on our progress.

Having a pure heart

A single mind and a pure heart belong together. The single mind is the product of a pure heart. I used to worry about the state of my heart because I knew it was very far from being pure. Still today, I echo the prayer of David. For how can I have a single purpose to glorify God when there is such duplicity in my heart? 'Create in me a pure heart, O God' should surely be the cry of a redeemed soul who comes face to face with the frightening potential of the old sinful nature.

If our passions are to be kept under control, we need God's help daily. Single-mindedness cannot be maintained by the power of the human will. It must arise from a divinely implanted desire to please God. The words of Jesus say it all: 'Watch and pray so that you will not fall into temptation. The spirit is willing, but the body is weak' (Matt. 26:41).

Keeping a pure heart is something we can cultivate by keeping our eyes fixed on Jesus. It is only by contemplating his glory by faith, that our minds and hearts are drawn to him in love. There is no greater privilege known to man than this. Those who are strangers to God's promises cannot have the faintest notion of the splendour of it. Sad to say, many believers fail at this point and, as a result, they lose a powerful incentive to maintain purity of heart. The more we exercise our faith in this way, the more loyal to him we shall become.

I am fully aware of the desire of some Christians to enjoy the privileges of the world to come before the time – like claiming perfect health and happiness right now – but these blessings are not yet. The evidence for those who have eyes to see, contradicts their claims. But we are privileged to have a little foretaste of the glory of Christ. We cannot fully comprehend it, even with the Spirit's aid, but our joyful and substantial expectation will make a vast improvement in our single-minded growth in holiness.

The reader should not go away with the idea that Christians should not have hobbies or secular interests. We all have work to do and it is right and proper that we should excel in our particular vocation. How can we shine like stars in the universe if we are not involved in the life of this world? Jesus himself was a carpenter. In any case, the world is in desperate need of godly builders, bankers, politicians and yes, godly ministers too.

The worldliness we are to avoid is spelled out for us by the apostle John: 'For everything in the world – the cravings of sinful man, the lust of the eyes and the boasting of what he has and does – comes not from the Father but from the world' (1 John 2:16). Our calling not to love the world is explained in terms of these three things.

Therefore, to use a Biblical metaphor, the task of every saint is to make every effort to strip off the clothes that hinder him in running the race. As the writer to the Hebrews says: 'Let us throw off everything that hinders and the sin that so easily entangles, and let us run with perseverance the race marked out for us' (Hebrews 12:1). That is being single-minded.

Must try harder

On a personal note, my school reports often contained comments about my lack of effort. Phrases like 'Frank must try harder' or similar, were written on several. I could not argue with it. I was very well aware that in class my mind was often elsewhere. Indeed, my attitude to learning did not change until God caught up with me. Then it changed dramatically for the better.

We have already seen that when it comes to the task of learning how to be holy we have from God all the help we need and the opportunity to make full use of it. 'His divine power has given us everything we need for life and godliness through our knowledge of him who called us by his own glory and goodness' (2 Peter 1:3). Again, the latter part of this verse shows that we were drawn to Christ by the power of his glory and his excellence.

Now notice what follows from this: 'For this very reason, make every effort to add to your faith goodness; and to goodness, knowledge; and to knowledge, self-control; and to self-control, perseverance; and to perseverance, godliness; and to godliness, brotherly kindness; and to brotherly kindness, love' (2 Peter 1:5-7). This has nothing to do with working *for* our salvation. We are saved by grace alone and we cannot contribute anything towards it. Christ did everything necessary. But now, we must work *out* our salvation.

Trying harder then, is the response we make to our great calling. Paul puts it beautifully: 'Continue to work out your salvation with fear and trembling, for it is God who works in you to will and to act according to his good purpose' (Phil. 2:12-13). The farmer goes out to plough his field and sow the seed but God sends the rain and causes the sun to shine. The farmer knows that the growth of the seed is a mystery. He knows that if he is lazy, there will be no harvest. But he also knows that if the rain doesn't fall and the sun doesn't shine, he is wasting his time.

In the same way, we have the responsibility to sow 'to please the Spirit' (Gal. 6:8). If we neglect any opportunity to do so, we shall not reap the benefits. It is a kind of divine partnership. If we are lazy, the joy of the Christian life will wane and our fellowship with God will be impaired. If, on the other hand, we are determined to use the means of grace to the full, God will richly bless us and make us a blessing to others.

Note. There are, of course, certain aspects of God's holiness that cannot be communicated to us. His holiness, for example, is transcendent. It exceeds anything known to man. His name is great and awesome (Ps. 99:3). Holiness is not something he acquired. It is not something added to his character as it is with us. Holiness is what he is. Obviously, we cannot be like God in this sense.

16. The ultimate good

God's power and ours

Power from above

Because I have just a little knowledge of computers, people who have even less sometimes ask me to fix their problems. A friend's laptop was not functioning properly. The machine was running slowly – taking far too long just to access the files. Editing was a tedious process. Connecting to the Internet was impossible. Imagine my chagrin when, after an hour's work, my friend, who knows nothing about computers, found the fault. It was a bad connection in the power supply.

The connection to the mains was being intermittently interrupted, so that the internal battery was flat and could not cope when the mains supply was broken. As soon as this was put right, the machine was back to speed. Not having a laptop, I never thought about the battery!

Christians are not machines, but without a constant supply of power, they too are useless. They are able to do some things on the power of their own batteries, so to speak, but to sanctify themselves is not one of them. The Holy Spirit is the only one who supplies the power to enable us to grow in holiness.

The new birth, as we saw earlier, is the work of the Holy Spirit. Just as dead men cannot move, so we were unable to make any move towards God. No one can give birth to himself. But once we have received the gift of new life in Christ, power from God is available to us.

This 'power' is not an impersonal force. It is the power of the Holy Spirit. Unlike the laptop with its battery power, the power of the Spirit never becomes our possession. This means that we cannot work independently of the supply. Contact with the source must be maintained at all times. We are still weak, but Christ's power is made perfect in weakness (2 Cor. 12:9).

An electric locomotive in the middle of a field with its pantograph waving about in the fresh air is a useless piece of machinery. Standing on a prepared track and in contact with the overhead power cable, it becomes very useful and profitable to its owner.

It is vitally important to get the order right. The new birth must come first. Trying to live a life that is pleasing to God prior to that vital transformation is just as hopeless as trying to get the locomotive in the field to move under it own power. This is why Jesus told religious Nicodemus that he must be born again (John 3:3). Living 'in accordance with the Spirit' (Rom 8:5) is the only kind of living that moves us to please God.

But, as we said earlier, although we cannot co-operate with the Spirit in our new birth, once we receive power from above, we become responsible to make the best use of it. This involves effort and discipline. In recent years, sections of the church have been making much of the work of the Holy Spirit and some of the trends have been unprofitable, to say the least. Almost unnoticed, teaching on the Spirit's work in our ongoing sanctification has been seriously neglected, if not forgotten.

Perhaps the day-to-day effort to make progress in what is a gradual and difficult process is not spectacular or immediate enough for some. The experience of the new birth may be instant and dramatic, as it was in my own case, but growing up into Christ takes a long time and is fraught with difficulties. Like the birth of a child, the delivery takes a very short time but the work involved in bringing the child up is long and hard. Our sanctification begins at the new birth and continues right through to the time of our death.

It also seems to have been overlooked in many quarters, that the Scriptures are the Spirit's tool in the task of making us like Jesus. Just as the driver of the locomotive, even though he has a prepared track, needs to follow his instructions carefully, so the saint has to keep close to the Word of God. The desire he plants in the human heart at the new birth is linked to the precepts of the Word of God. Just as we 'have been born again, not of perishable seed, but of imperishable, through the living and enduring word of God' (1 Peter 1:23), so we grow by the same principle. The Word of God must become the rule by which we live.

The Word of God is our rule as it stands. We have nothing to do with those critics who try to weaken the challenge of the Word and rob the gospel of its power (Rom. 1:16). They stand in the tradition of Satan and ask 'did God really say...? (Gen. 3:1). Nor are we party to those who, like the Pharisees, want to add to God's commands. 'Do not add to his words, or he will rebuke you and prove you a liar' (Prov. 30:6). Either way leads to derailment.

The ultimate good

Earlier, I pointed briefly to Romans 8:28-29 to show what our ultimate good really is. We now need to go a little more deeply into these important verses. It is essential that we understand them: 'And we know that in all things God works for the good of those who love him, who have been called according to his purpose. For those God foreknew he also predestined to be conformed to the image of his Son, that he might be the firstborn among many brothers.'

To their cost, many believers take verse 28 out of its context. They seem to think that God is promising them a smooth ride through life. In my early days as a Christian, I often saw the verse hanging on someone's wall and my elders frequently quoted it. When anything seemed to go wrong – being brought up on the Authorised Version – they would say, 'Don't worry, all things work together for good.' What follows in verse 29 was ignored and, as a result, I too began to entertain the foolish notion that the Christian life is a bed of roses.

The meaning of the word 'good' in verse 28 is to be found in verse 29. It points forward to our final destiny when we shall be like Jesus in his glorious perfection. There can be no greater good than this. Therefore, when we take the two verses in their context, we see at once what Paul is saying. In all things, God works towards making those who love him more and more like Jesus, because they are predestined to be conformed to the image of Christ. It is not enough to say that we are predestined to go to heaven when we die. We are predestined to holiness as a necessary preparation for heaven.

The trials may not seem very good at the time, but God uses the nasty experiences as well as the pleasant ones to knock us into shape. We should not entertain the idea that believers are immune from severe trials. Nor should we pretend that we are not deeply affected by them. The fact is, we would not benefit from them without the anguish they cause. Purifying the character can be a painful business at times.

It will be seen that the past, present and future dimensions of the Christian life are all contained in these two verses. In the past, God predestined us to be like Jesus. In the present, God is at work making sure that our circumstances serve his purpose for us. In the future, God will achieve his aim. 'Without holiness no-one will see the Lord' (Heb. 12:14).

Before moving on, we need to look more closely at the word 'foreknew' as Paul uses it. The necessity arises because some believers try to explain predestination away by saying that God merely foresaw who would believe and decided to predestine them. But this does not make sense. It puts the initiative back with us – the very opposite of what Paul is saying. If we make the first move, how can God be the one who predestines us? The idea that he predestined us because he saw in advance that we would, of our own volition, believe and strive to be like Jesus is absurd. Without him, we can do nothing. No, the word 'foreknew' means that God knew every one of his saints, in person, before the world was made.

Bogus holiness

As we have seen, true holiness has nothing to do with that commendable goodness and kindness which many unbelievers demonstrate in their lives. Human goodness is not godliness. Any improvement in a person's morals is to be welcomed, but if such improvement is not due to a living relationship with God, it has nothing whatever to do with true holiness.

Therefore, holiness cannot be understood except in relation to God himself. Holiness is godliness, and those who do not know God cannot be godly, no matter how 'good' they are. Even when the Bible refers to things like holy ground (Exod. 3:5), sacred garments (Exod. 28:2) and the Holy Place (Exod. 26:33) they are only so described because of their association with God.

Without the Holy Spirit, true holiness will never be realised by anyone. We shall come back to this vital subject a little later.

Free will?

Many saints believe it is possible to fall from grace and be lost. They see professing Christians falling into sin and 'losing their faith' and this confirms their belief. They also see others making mistakes, like entering into wrong relationships, so that their spiritual growth comes to a standstill. From this, they draw the conclusion that the responsibility to grow in grace is entirely theirs. Otherwise, they would not be free.

Believers of this persuasion suffer heavy loss. Working on the principle that everything depends on them, they forfeit one of the greatest blessings of the Christian life. They know nothing of the confident assurance that an inheritance awaits us that can 'never perish, spoil or fade – kept in heaven for you, who through faith are shielded by God's power until the coming of the salvation that is ready to be revealed in the last time' (1 Peter 1:4-5). The word 'kept' means reserved. It is already set aside for our future enjoyment.

Paul makes the same point: 'Having believed, you were marked in him with a seal, the promised Holy Spirit, who is a deposit guaranteeing our inheritance' (Eph. 1:13-14). 'And do not grieve the Holy Spirit of God with whom you were sealed for the day of redemption' (Eph. 4:30). The seal of God's Spirit marks us as God's property and guarantees our security.

In most cases, the mistaken views mentioned above are the consequence of a false understanding of the nature of human free-will. It is common today for believers to think and speak of their faith as if they were the ones who initiated it. The ability to choose Christ did not come from above but was theirs by right! It is the Corinthian error all over again: 'What do you have that you did not receive? And if you did receive it, why do you boast as though you did not?' (1 Cor. 4:7).

Everything that makes me different from others, including all the gifts of God's abundant grace, comes from God. My conversion, my calling, my attainments and my inheritance in heaven are all due to God's goodness to me. 'But by the grace of God I am what I am, and his grace to me was not without effect' (1 Cor. 15:10).

A friend put this question to me: 'Do you not agree with me that we can say 'no' to God?' The aim of the questioner was to prove to me that everyone has free will to choose or to reject Christ.

Well, of course we can say 'no' to God. In our natural condition that is all we can say. The real question is, 'Can we say "yes"?' Unless God draws us to himself, the answer is 'no' (John 6:44).

The teaching that fallen human nature has the ability to choose what is spiritually beneficial is not to be found anywhere in Holy Scripture. The overwhelming testimony of the Bible is that in our natural condition we are slaves to sin. Why? Because 'the sinful mind is hostile to God. It does not submit to God's law, nor can it do so. Those controlled by the sinful nature cannot please God' (Rom. 8:7-8).

Again, the idea that all people have faith if only they would have the sense to use it finds no support in the Scriptures. Paul clearly teaches that faith is God's gift and not everyone has it (Eph. 2:8; 2 Thess. 3:2). In our natural condition, we had freedom to do many things within limits, but choosing Christ was not one of them. Before our conversion to Christ, we were cut off from the source of spiritual life and there was nothing we could do about it. Free-will to choose Christ is an illusion.

Believers who fail to understand this will not find it easy to get rid of the dangerous idea that they are in control of their own destiny. They will also be handicapped in their spiritual growth. However, once we understand that the initiative belongs to God, everything falls into place. We see the call to holiness as coming from God, along with the ability to achieve it. It all becomes part of God's sovereign plan for us.

As far back as the fifth century, Augustine – a man before his time – posed these rhetorical questions: 'Do we unite ourselves to God without God's help, in order that we may receive his help after we have entered into union with him? What great gift, what equal gift, could grace itself give a person, if he has – already, without grace – been able to make himself one spirit with the Lord, by no other power than his own free will?' (Nicene and Post-Nicene Fathers: Series I/Volume V/On the Grace of Christ, and on Original Sin/On the Grace of Christ/Chapter 24.)

If the answer to Augustine's first question is 'yes', the answer to the second is 'none'. This is the mistake made by many. If, however, we answer 'no' to the first, then we accept that we are just as dependent on God for his help in our growth in holiness as we were for our new birth.

I have known one or two Christians in my lifetime who were determined not to get married. They made a deliberate choice. Perhaps they preferred to have freedom and jingling pockets rather than the responsibility of marriage. Then, out of the blue, so to speak, a very attractive and eligible member of the opposite sex appeared and they fell head-over-heels in love.

Suddenly, there was nothing else in the world they wanted more than to marry the one they loved. Did they marry against their will? Were they forced into it? Of course not. Did they change their minds? Yes they did. They married because they wanted to. That very attractive person of the opposite sex had the effect of changing the will!

Now if that happens on the human level, how much more on the divine? Does God reveal Jesus to people who are determined not to have anything to do with him? Of course he does. Do they then love him against their will? Not at all. When God reveals the beauty of Jesus to them, the desire to know him becomes irresistible.

The Scriptures are unambiguous and incontrovertible. To young Timothy Paul says, God 'has saved us and called us to a holy life – not because of anything we have done but because of his own purpose and grace. This grace was given us in Christ Jesus before the beginning of time... (2 Tim. 1:9). To the church in Ephesus, the apostle writes: 'In him we were also chosen, having been predestined according to the plan of him who works out everything in conformity with the purpose of his will' (Eph 1:11). Surely there cannot be any doubt about Paul's meaning.

The process of sanctification begins as soon as God calls us. In other words, as soon as we become saints in name, we begin to become saints in character. To understand that this is God's purpose is very important. Believers who remain ignorant of it are at a serious disadvantage. Not having any clear idea why God saved them, they wander through life with no apparent aim. The spiritual poverty and lack of direction among believers today is due mainly to ignorance on this point.

As for those who fall away, if they are truly God's children he will bring them back from the wilderness and set their feet back on the right path. If they are not God's children, they were not really on the right path in the first place.

We conclude, then, that the will to choose what is beneficial to our spiritual health and prosperity is the gift of God. Jesus Christ is the one who sets us free from slavery to sin and gives us the ability to co-operate with the Spirit of God in our progress in holy living. To deny this, is to malign the grace of God.

17. The saints' suffering

How the saints are purified

The value of suffering

Many have addressed the problem of suffering. Perhaps, the best-known book on the subject is C. S. Lewis's *The Problem of Pain* (Fount, 1940). It is a scholarly attempt to reconcile suffering with the love of God. Many regard the book as a classic, but, as we would expect, it does not satisfy everyone.

The reader may be familiar with the argument of the sceptics. If God were almighty and loving, he would not allow people to suffer as they do. Therefore, the existence of suffering proves that he is either not almighty or not loving or both. We reject such a superficial conclusion.

Suffering has great value for the saints. It tests our sincerity and separates the genuine believers from the false. In the parable of the soils, Jesus told us that the seed sown on the rocky ground represents the 'believer' who lasts only a short time. He receives the word with joy but 'When trouble or persecution comes because of the word, he quickly falls away' (Matt. 13:20-21).

The main value and purpose of suffering for the saints is the development of their saintliness – a fact that is often overlooked today. The Psalmist recognised this: 'Before I was afflicted I went astray, but now I obey your word' (Ps. 119:67). 'It was good for me to be afflicted, so that I might learn your decrees' (Ps. 119:71). He even regarded his suffering as a token of God's faithfulness: 'I know, O Lord, that your laws are righteous, and in faithfulness you have afflicted me' (Ps. 119:75). This is how every saint should regard suffering.

We learn from the Scriptures that suffering formed no part of God's original creation. Nor will it feature in the new creation (Rev. 21:4). Christ's suffering on the cross has made sure of that. But in the meantime, the saints must endure suffering because it is a necessary preparation for the glory to come. It must take precedence over their present comfort for the simple reason that our holiness is more important to God than our earthly happiness.

Unless we have foolishly brought the suffering on ourselves, it should never be seen as a punishment. God's purpose in our affliction is to purify us, and to mould our character after the pattern of our Saviour. If Jesus himself 'learned obedience from what he suffered' (Heb. 5:8), how much more needful it is for us.

Such suffering is not confined to the anguish we experience because of the hostility of this present world. It includes the common sorrows of this life – the tragedy of 'accidents', the loss of those we have loved, and the thousand and one things that go wrong with our mortal bodies, causing pain and disability. For the believer such common suffering is hallowed because it becomes a partaking of Christ's suffering.

In my pulpit ministry, I always stressed the divine purpose of suffering in the life of a believer. Because of this, I once found myself in the unusual position of having to defend myself against another clergyman whose church was a few miles away. Someone in my congregation was reporting the details of my sermon to him, and as a result, he took the liberty of writing to me to set me right.

His position was clear. He insisted that it is never God's will for Christians to suffer! You may well wonder which Bible he was reading. The Scriptures could not be clearer on the subject.

God told Ananias to go to the house where the newly converted Saul of Tarsus was residing. This was the message Ananias was to convey: 'Go! This man is my chosen instrument to carry my name before the Gentiles and their kings and before the people of Israel. I will show him how much he must suffer for my name' (Acts 9:15-16).

Let no-one say that Paul was a special case. Every saint must suffer. 'A righteous man may have many troubles,' says the Psalmist, 'but the LORD delivers him from them all' (Ps. 34:19). Paul confirms this: 'In fact, everyone who wants to live a godly life in Christ Jesus will be persecuted' (2 Tim. 3:12).

Although the Scriptures sometimes speak of Satan as the source of suffering, especially physical, it is always made clear that he cannot touch us unless our God permits it. It was so with Job (Job 1). It was so with Paul, who said: 'To keep me from becoming conceited because of these surpassingly great revelations, there was given me a thorn in my flesh, a messenger of Satan, to torment me' (2 Cor. 12:7).

Now who would credit Satan with such a motive for tormenting Paul? Our adversary is not the slightest bit interested in keeping the saints humble. God was using Satan as a tool to prevent Paul from becoming conceited. We too may be sure that Satan cannot cause us to suffer, except by divine permission.

Suffering, therefore, whatever its source, is an instrument God uses to good effect in the lives of his saints. Irresponsible preachers may paint a rosy picture of the life of a Christian, in the hope that more people will respond to the gospel, but it is a false picture. Christians may often suffer more, not less, than others. To tell any believer that it is not God's will for him to suffer is irresponsible. To rebuke the believer's suffering in the name of Jesus, as is sometimes done, is even worse.

The apostles did not deceive young believers in this way. They knew better. We read that Paul and Barnabas 'returned to Lystra, Iconium and Antioch, strengthening the disciples and encouraging them to remain true to the faith. "We must go through many hardships to enter the kingdom of God," they said' (Acts 14:21-22).

Now I wonder how many ministers today would try to encourage young believers by telling them that they must suffer? I know there are many 'evangelists' out there who offer prosperity and perfect health. But here we have it, straight from the apostles: 'We must go through many hardships'! The words 'we must' indicate that God has so ordained it.

I remember suffering stiff and sustained opposition from a group of self-righteous church folk, some of whom would stop at nothing to blacken my character. A goodly number of new converts were coming into the church at the time and they too came under fire. I feared for them. How would they cope with such insidious persecution from people who claimed to be Christians? I need not have worried. Instead of being cowed, they grew visibly in strength and character.

Yes, I should have known better. After all, is this not what the apostle Peter tells us? Speaking of the salvation of his readers, he says: 'In this you greatly rejoice, though now for a little while you may have had to suffer grief in all kinds of trials.' Now notice carefully what follows: 'These have come so that your faith – of greater worth than gold, which perishes even though refined by fire – may be proved genuine and may result in praise, glory and honour when Jesus Christ is revealed' (1 Peter 1:6-7).

Keeping the vision clear

Do you know the story of Elisha's servant Gehazi? He went out early one morning and had the fright of his life. He saw the armies of Israel's enemies surrounding the city. 'Oh, my lord, what shall we do?' Gehazi asked Elisha. 'Don't be afraid,' Elisha answered. 'Those who are with us are more than those who are with them.'

Apparently, this did not satisfy the servant because Elisha went on to pray, 'O LORD, open his eyes so that he may see.' Then, the servant's eyes were opened and 'he looked and saw the hills full of horses and chariots of fire all around Elisha' (2 Kings 6:15-17).

Frequently, restricted vision is the cause of fear. So it was with the servant Gehazi. He had not yet learned that the battle is the Lord's and that he is able to deliver his faithful servants from apparently impossible situations. Mind you, I cannot think badly of the servant because there have been times in my life when I have suffered from limited vision, feeling that all is lost and help is not forthcoming. There have been times when I discovered that my eyes were not 'fixed on Jesus' as they should have been. Instead of learning to trust the Lord more and develop spiritually, I became fearful and discouraged. Thankfully, the Lord still has lessons to teach us even when we fail. But how much better to keep our vision clear!

Every saint is tested. It may be a broken relationship, a chronic illness, persecution of some kind, or just sheer weariness with the task in hand. At the time, we may not understand what is happening to us. Later on, we see that the Lord used the experience to mould our character. 'No discipline seems pleasant at the time, but painful. Later on, however, it produces a harvest of righteousness and peace for those who have been trained by it' (Heb. 12:11).

Even when we are not under pressure, we can be blind to the fact that God is at work behind the apparently uneventful scene. The daily routine can dull our vision of Jesus just as much as the severe trials. We need to pray regularly that God will keep us on our toes so that we are quick to detect when the glory is fading and our progress slowing down.

At these times, it is very important that we should be careful about our study of the Scriptures and our prayers. At times when we may not feel like it, it is vitally important to keep up the discipline. There is no better way of keeping all those chariots of fire in clear focus. If we are unable to do this because of physical weakness through illness, we should try to get someone else to read the Word to us and intercede for us. In an ideal situation, the 'elders of the church' whom James advises us to call, would be the best people (James 5:14). But where this is not the case, the assistance of any older and wiser believer is better than none at all.

Sharing Christ's suffering

If we have brought suffering on ourselves, we need to repent and seek God's mercy and forgiveness. Such suffering forms no part of Christ's suffering. If I, as a diabetic, were to eat rich cream cakes or sticky toffee pudding every day, or refuse to inject the appropriate dose of insulin, I would only have myself to blame if I became sick.

Mental suffering may also be self-inflicted. I think of Christians I have known who suffered for years because of an unkind remark they made but are too proud to apologise. If, on the contrary, we suffer because of someone else's loose tongue, we need to learn how to have a forgiving spirit. If we fail at this point and allow bitterness to enter, the pain becomes self-inflicted. Either way, we need to remember that our forgiveness by God is conditional on our forgiveness of others (Matt. 6:15).

Some believers argue that because God does not forgive the sinner unless he repents, we ought to do the same. Obviously, until the other party repents, the healing of the broken relationship cannot take place. But surely, if the offended party does not show a forgiving spirit, the offender is far less likely to repent. Since Jesus adopted a forgiving spirit towards his persecutors and asked his father to forgive them (Luke 23:34), we should follow his example.

An unforgiving spirit in the saints brings spiritual growth to a halt. It sours our relationship with God. It deprives us of the blessings that would otherwise accompany our suffering. 'If you are insulted because of the name of Christ', says Peter, 'you are blessed, for the spirit of glory and of God rests on you' (1 Peter 4:14).

Suffering must also be seen as a reminder of our mortality. We must use it to keep the shortness of life in focus. This will help us to fix our eyes on the glory of our risen and ascended Saviour. It will also assist us in adopting the right attitude to our worldly possessions and to lay up treasure in heaven.

Jesus pronounces people blessed who are insulted, persecuted and falsely accused because of righteousness (Matt. 5:10-11). If we think we are suffering for this reason, the first thing to do is to make sure that this is indeed the case. The saints can sometimes be unfeeling, even cutting, in their defence of what is right, and then they wonder why they suffer a reaction. The first duty of every saint who believes he is being persecuted for the sake of righteousness is to ask himself some searching questions. Have I done anything to bring this on myself? Have I been overbearing or rude in my witness? Did I fail to show compassion? Am I being stubborn? Have I been 'a meddler' (1 Peter 4:15)?

If we are convinced that we are suffering for the cause of righteousness, our second duty is to realise that this is our calling. As Paul says to the saints in Philippi: 'For it has been granted to you on behalf of Christ not only to believe on him, but also to suffer for him' (Phil. 1:29). To accept this without a murmur brings many blessings, not least a deepening assurance that God is at work in our lives, preparing us for the glory to come.

'Dear friends, do not be surprised at the painful trial you are suffering, as though something strange were happening to you. But rejoice that you participate in the sufferings of Christ, so that you may be overjoyed when his glory is revealed' (1 Peter 4:12-13). If we acknowledge that the suffering is from God and serves his purpose of proving us, the benefits are both present and future. We are able to rejoice here and now that we have the privilege of participating in the sufferings of Christ, and we shall be the more overjoyed when his glory is revealed.

We shall also have the further benefit of being a blessing to others. Writing to the Corinthians, Paul says: 'For just as the sufferings of Christ flow over into our lives, so also through Christ our comfort overflows' (2 Cor. 1:5). In spite of the suffering, the comfort we enjoy is so great that it overflows to others in their distress.

For me, the most challenging verse of the apostolic writings on this subject is Colossians 1:24: 'Now I rejoice in what was suffered for you, and I fill up in my flesh what is still lacking in regard to Christ's afflictions, for the sake of his body, which is the church.' These words cannot imply that Christ's suffering for our sins needs supplementing, as some would have it. The sufferings of Christ for our redemption are complete and sufficient for the sins of the whole world.

Some take the view that 'what is still lacking in regard to Christ's afflictions' refers to the sufferings Christ endured for the building up of the church. Obviously, they were not complete because we, his servants, have to suffer with him for the same reason. Yet others think of it in terms of Christ's suffering in Paul as he laboured to build the church.

This is not as unlikely as it may seem. When God stopped Saul of Tarsus in his tracks on the Damascus Road when he was determined to persecute the church, what did Jesus say to him? Did he say, 'Why are you persecuting my church?' Not at all. Note his words carefully: 'Saul, Saul, why do you persecute me?' (Acts 9:4). The sufferings of the church that Saul was persecuting were also the sufferings of Christ.

The words are challenging because, although I can now rejoice that I have been privileged to suffer with Christ in the building of the church, I found it extremely difficult at the time. Close friends would tell me this was because I have a sensitive nature. I appreciate their kindness, but to excuse myself on this basis would be quite wrong. At least, my experience helps me to understand what a profound statement Paul made when he spoke of sharing Christ's sufferings.

One thing is certain – if we are to be made more like Jesus, we must know something of the fellowship of his sufferings. No doubt, Paul rejoiced in his sufferings because he knew that they were intended for his own progress towards Christ-likeness. Here is his desire: 'I want to know Christ and the power of his resurrection and the fellowship of sharing in his sufferings, becoming like him in his death…' (Phil. 3:10). May it also be ours.

18. The saints' struggle

With whom are the saints fighting?

A holy war

Just imagine being at war for over a hundred years! From 1337 to 1453, England and France were at war. The main cause of the struggle was the claim of English Kings to the French throne. The war was divided into three phases. The first phase, lasting twenty-three years from 1337 to 1360, is known as the Edwardian War. The second phase from 1369 to 1389. was called the Caroline War after Charles V of France. The Lancastrian War (1415-1429) came third. It started when the English king Henry V invaded Normandy. Even though there were periods of peace, the name *The Hundred Years' War* was given to the entire period by later historians.

If the saints were to live for a hundred years, the war against the world, the flesh and the devil would also be a hundred years' war. But there would be no interludes of peace. Every saint is fighting this war and it will last as long as he is lives. That is to say, it will last from the time of his conversion to the day of his death.

There will be times when the fight is not so fierce but making peace, even temporary peace, with our enemy is out of the question. The peace comes only when we leave this body. For me, at the time of writing, it has already been a seventy years' war – with no peace breaks!

A woman who was having a tough time fighting against temptation once said to me, 'It's OK for you, you are a minister'! Evidently, she thought that being set apart for a holy purpose protected me from the temptations experienced by ordinary people. I had to explain to her that every true believer, whatever his vocation, never stops fighting against temptation. No minister of the gospel is immune. Indeed, there are particular temptations that go with the job.

Before God drew us to himself, the world did not hate us. Nor did our sinful nature trouble us much. Satan was content to leave us alone. The moment Christ took possession of us, everything changed. The world's love turned to hatred, our sinful nature began to plague us and Satan, being robbed of his influence, began to attack us from all angles.

Our adversaries

The other reason why there are no periods of peace in the Christian war is that our adversaries never sue for peace. Nor do they lay down their arms. As mentioned above, they are often referred to as 'the world, the flesh and the devil'. In today's world, these titles will not make sense to many, so let me explain what they mean, and how and why they are antagonistic towards us.

1. The world

The 'world' in this context stands for the unbelieving people of the world. As we saw just now, they are naturally hostile to God (Rom. 8:7) and, therefore, hostile to God's children as well. Jesus warned his disciples: 'If the world hates you, keep in mind that it hated me first. If you belonged to the world, it would love you as its own. As it is, you do not belong to the world, but I have chosen you out of the world. That is why the world hates you' (John 15:18-19).

All through history the saints have been persecuted for the simple reason that they do not belong to this world anymore. They belong to the Lord Jesus Christ.

It is important to remember that the Bible uses the word 'world' in different senses. Because of this, it sometimes causes confusion. We are told, for example, in John 3:16 that God loved the world. But the apostle John says: 'Do not love the world or anything in the world' (1 John 2:15). There is no contradiction. God loved the world in the sense that he set his love on people all over the world – people from every tribe and nation –'a great multitude that no-one could count, from every nation, tribe, people and language' (Rev. 7:9).

Every single one of them, whether they lived in the shanty towns of South Africa or the mansions of Beverley Hills, is a sinner saved by grace. And every one had a natural hostility towards God. It is in this sense that Jesus is 'the Saviour of the world' (1 John 4:14).

The apostle John warns us against the evil and hostility of godless society. Indeed, he tells us what he means by 'the world'. He defines it as 'the cravings of sinful man, the lust of his eyes and the boasting of what he has and does' (1 John 2:16). He is not telling us to treat the antagonistic people of the world as they treat us. On the contrary, we are to love them. But at the same time we are to take care that we do not throw our lot in with them or love any of the things they love.

All saints are to be like their Lord in this matter. 'When they hurled their insults at him, he did not retaliate.' We should not deserve to be persecuted any more than Jesus did. We should take it patiently and follow the example of Jesus who 'entrusted himself to him who judges justly' (1 Peter 2:23).

2. The flesh

In the New Testament the word 'flesh' is sometimes used just as we would use it, to refer to the body. In 1 Cor. 15:39 for example, the apostle Paul says: 'All flesh is not the same: Men have one kind of flesh, animals have another, birds another and fish another.' This is the meaning we usually attach to the word today.

But Paul also uses the word to refer to the sinful nature of mankind. Indeed, to help readers understand, where the word is used in this sense, the New International Version uses the term 'sinful nature' rather than the world 'flesh'. For example, 'All of us also lived among them at one time, gratifying the cravings of our sinful nature and following its desires and thoughts' (Eph. 2:3).

The 'flesh' then, as Paul often uses it, is the opposite of our new nature from God. In Romans 7:25, the apostle makes a clear distinction between his old sinful nature and his new nature: 'So then, I myself [the new Paul] in my mind am a slave to God's law. But in the sinful nature [the old Paul] a slave to the law of sin.' Versions of the New Testament that are concerned to follow the Greek text closely will, of course, still use the word 'flesh'.

Surprisingly, the apostle tends to disown his old sinful nature altogether: 'Now if I do what I do not want to do, it is no longer I who do it, but it is sin living in me that does it' (Rom. 7:20). He is saying that when his sinful nature causes him to sin, the new Paul strongly disapproves of it. So much so, that it is no longer Paul who does it! The apostle is not trying to avoid responsibility. He is now so identified with his new nature that the sins of the old bring self-condemnation and genuine repentance. Indeed, the believer who claims to be able to subdue the old nature entirely, is merely showing his ignorance.

It is only fair to say that many Bible commentators do not accept the latter part of Romans 7 as an account of Paul's experience as a Christian. They cannot accept that a true Christian would ever say that he is a slave to the law of sin. How can a believer, they ask, be a slave to sin?

We cannot go into detail of the arguments for and against here, but for me, the evidence that Paul is referring to his personal experience – his day-to-day struggle with sin as a child of God – is overwhelming. Writing on the same subject in Gal. 5:17, he says: 'For the sinful nature desires what is contrary to the Spirit, and the Spirit what is contrary to the sinful nature. They are in conflict with each other, so that you do not do what you want.' That Paul is here referring to the saints' normal Christian experience can hardly be disputed.

I have no hesitation in saying that Paul's words describe my experience perfectly. I heartily echo his thanksgiving that one day the Lord Christ will rescue me from this body of death (Rom. 7:24-25), but in the meantime I have no illusions about the evil potential of my sinful nature.

In war, knowledge of the enemy's strength and strategy is vital. To know the capacity of the sinful nature to deceive us, makes us more dependent on God's power. Failure to recognise it makes us careless and leaves us in a vulnerable position. King David of Israel delighted in God's Word as much as any man, but he fell into the monstrous sins of adultery and murder. The story stands as a warning to us.

When I was young in the faith, I remember hearing a talk on this subject. An illustration used by the speaker has remained with me ever since. It runs something like this: A new convert was explaining the difference Christ had made in her life. 'When Satan knocked on the door of my heart', she said, 'I would open the door but he always pushed his way in. I was not strong enough to keep him out. Now, when he knocks, I ask Jesus to answer the door. Satan always runs away muttering something about having come to the wrong house.'

The illustration would fit well into the next section on our fight against Satan. I put it here to illustrate the importance of divine assistance in preventing Satan's appeal to our sinful nature from succeeding. Jesus did not have a sinful nature. That is why he said, 'the prince of this world is coming. He has no hold on me...' (John 14:30). Not so with us. Christ alone is our defence.

Therefore, now that we have the Spirit of God living in us, our sinful nature no longer has free reign. It has received a fatal blow so that our ultimate victory over it is secured. 'For sin shall not be your master, because you are not under law but under grace' (Rom. 6:14). Nevertheless, its continuing presence means that our hearts are never perfectly inclined to do the will of God.

Now, God expects us to co-operate with him, using the strength he gives us. This is why Paul tells us to count ourselves 'dead to sin but alive to God in Christ Jesus'. We are solemnly charged not to allow sin to reign in our mortal bodies, not to obey its evil desires (Rom 6:11-12). The New Testament teems with similar injunctions: 'Hate what is evil; cling to what is good' (Rom. 12:9). 'Be careful to do what is right in the eyes of everybody' (Rom 12:17). 'Let us not become weary in doing good…' (Gal. 6:9).

Before we move on, there are a couple of apparent contradictions in the apostle's teaching that we need to resolve. We looked briefly at the first in chapter eight. In Gal. 5:24, Paul tells us that believers 'have crucified the sinful nature with its passions and desires'. Yet in Col 3:5 he says, 'Put to death, therefore, whatever belongs to your earthly nature: sexual immorality, impurity, lust, evil desires and greed, which is idolatry.' In the first text, he seems to be telling us that our sinful nature is dead. In the second, he is telling us it is very much alive. So are we dead to sin or not?

Second, the purpose of Christ's death is said to be the utter destruction of our sinful nature. This is what Paul meant when he said, 'I have been crucified with Christ and I no longer live, but Christ lives in me. The life I live in the body, I live by faith in the Son of God who loved me and gave himself for me' (Gal. 2:20). This is God's work in us. In Galatians 5:24, however, the apostle says that *we* have crucified the sinful nature. So whose work is it, God's or ours?

In answer to the first apparent contradiction, we do not doubt that we have been united with Christ in his death. 'For we know that our old self was crucified with him so that the body of sin might be done away with [or 'rendered powerless', NIV footnote], that we should no longer be slaves to sin' (Rom. 6:5-6). This means that, as God's elect, our sinful nature received a fatal blow at the cross from which it will never recover. But death by crucifixion is slow and painful.

Therefore, the answer to the question, 'are we dead to sin or not?', is both 'yes' and 'no'. We are dead in the sense that sin can never again take control of us. The answer to the second question, 'is it God's work or ours?' is 'both'. God has crucified our old nature and now he expects us to confirm this by decisively rejecting it. In other words, we should co-operate with God in assisting the crucified body of sin to die.

Every believer has, or should have the joy of knowing that he is on the victory side. His deliverance from the power and penalty of sin is complete right now. He does not have to wait to see how he fares in the future. But as long as he is in this body, he cannot sit back and assume the fight against sin is over. He is still prone to temptation.

It helps me to think of the old 'me' hanging on a cross. I know death is certain, but it is taking longer than I expected. Therefore, I must speed up the process. The new 'me' must ensure that I do not do anything that might temporarily revive the crucified body. I must ignore its demands. To change the metaphor, if I am tempted to sin, I must knock it on the head before it develops. This is the process Paul is referring to in Rom. 8:13, 'but if by the Spirit you put to death the misdeeds of the body, you will live'. (The reader may like to glance back to chapter 9 where we looked at the role of God's Word in this task.)

The first part of the above verse: 'If you live according to the sinful nature, you will die…' (Rom. 8:13), describes the activity of those who have their minds set on what the sinful nature desires (Rom. 8:5). They can do no other. They remain in the same state we were in before God called us to himself, 'dead in trespasses and sins' (Eph 2:1). But now, we put the deeds of the old nature to death 'by the Spirit'. This means, incidentally, that we are still unable to take any credit for the progress we make.

Our obligation is summed up in the verses partially quoted above: 'Put to death, therefore, whatever belongs to your earthly nature: sexual immorality, impurity, lust, evil desires and greed, which is idolatry. Because of these, the wrath of God is coming. You used to walk in these ways, in the life you once lived. But now you must rid yourselves of all such things as these: anger, rage, malice, slander and filthy language from your lips' (Col. 3:5-8).

3. The devil

The third enemy is the devil. When I was a child few people believed in the existence of Satan, but in more recent times, he has come back into prominence. A few years ago, according to some believers, he was appearing round every corner!

The first thing we need to understand is that Satan has no power except by divine permission. Whether he knows it or not, Satan is God's tool, to be used to serve his purpose as he sees fit. Scripture leaves us in no doubt that he is a real person and not merely an evil influence, but with the power given to us by the Holy Spirit we are able to outwit him.

Some readers may have difficulty with the notion that God uses evil to bring good. This problem has exercised many great minds down the years. If God created evil, then how can he hate it? Everything he made is good. But if someone else created evil, we are faced with a problem. There must be a conflict between good and evil so how can we know who is going to win?

Back in the fifth century, Augustine of Hippo (354-430) was deeply troubled by this problem. Listen to his agonising comments in my simplified and abbreviated version: 'Could evil exist contrary to God's will? If it has always been there, why did he allow it to remain dormant for so long and then make something out of it? If the Almighty wanted to create something, would he not have chosen to get rid of evil first? ….He would not be all-powerful if he couldn't create something good without the assistance of what had not been created by him. These problems troubled me – I didn't want to die before I had discovered the truth' (*Augustine's Confessions*, Book 7, Chapter 5).

Augustine concluded that God preferred to bring good out of evil rather than to get rid of evil altogether. If this were not the case, the sanctification of the saints would be impossible. They would never be tested by temptation and trials and the purifying effect of suffering would be lost. What Satan did to Job (with divine permission) was evil. He lost his family, his possessions and his health. But God used the evil to mould Job's character, so that he was able to say: 'But he knows the way that I take; when he has tested me, I will come forth as gold' (Job 23:10). The trial, like a furnace, will burn away all that is not pure gold.

Isaiah makes a direct reference to Satan being cast down when he says: 'How you have fallen from heaven O morning star, son of the dawn! You have been cast down to the earth, you who once laid low the nations. You said in your heart, "I will ascend to heaven; I will raise my throne above the stars of God"' (Isaiah 14:12-13). I once heard Donald Grey Barnhouse say, commenting on this passage: 'Satan did not just want to share God's throne; rather he wanted him to move over.'

Jesus too referred to the time when Satan was cast down to encourage his disciples not to fear him: 'I saw Satan fall like lightning from heaven' (Luke 10:18). We conclude from this that although Satan is still waging war against the saints, he is fighting a losing battle and he knows it.

Writing to the Corinthians on the importance of forgiveness, Paul adds these words: '…in order that Satan might not outwit us. For we are not unaware of his schemes' (2 Cor. 2:11). Clearly then, Satan is a person who is constantly plotting against the saints. Our task is to prevent him from getting a foothold, and that calls for constant vigilance.

Peter too speaks of the purpose of trials in the life of the saints: '...now for a little while you may have had to suffer grief in all kinds of trials. These have come so that your faith – of greater worth than gold, which perishes even though refined by fire – may be proved genuine' (1 Peter 1:6-7). Like Job, the apostle is talking about trials that come from without rather than within. They do cause us grief, but they are essential for the proof of our faith. Just as the furnace burns up the dross and leaves the gold, so trials have a destructive effect on the old nature and reveal the beauty and sincerity of the new.

In the above passage, Peter does not mention Satan although he may well have a hand in these trials. We may learn from this that it is not necessary to try and determine what role Satan plays in our trials. It serves no useful purpose.

The wonderful truth about all this is that the fight against the world, the flesh and the devil is essential for the believer's growth in holiness. As James says: 'Blessed is the man who perseveres under trial, because when he has stood the test, he will receive the crown of life that God has promised to those who love him' (James 1:12). The word 'trial' in this verse is the word for temptation, the word used by the older versions.

Praying and giving

Christians never find it easy to establish set patterns of daily prayer and regular Christian giving. We would all agree that believers who do not pray much don't grow much, and those who do not give do not prosper. Generosity and holiness are like twins. It is impossible to be holy, mean and prayerless all at the same time.

When I say that believers who do not give do not prosper, I am not advocating the so-called 'prosperity doctrine' – the teaching that generous giving is a way of getting rich. I use the word 'prosper' in a much wider sense. 'A generous man will himself be blessed' (Prov. 22:9). Paul too, reminds us that 'Whoever sows sparingly will also reap sparingly, and whoever sows generously will also reap generously ... God is able to make all grace abound to you, so that in all things at all times, having all that you need, you will abound in every good work' (2 Cor. 9:6,8). If I give with a view to getting rich, my motives are all wrong.

Nevertheless, Scripture does teach that generosity does not pose any risk to our financial security. 'One man gives freely, yet gains even more; another withholds unduly, but comes to poverty' (Prov. 11:24). In any case, we need to remember that everything we have and are is the Lord's.

Many saints adopt the Old Testament principle of tithing – giving a tenth of their income (Lev. 27:32). The New Testament instructions do not mention tithing, the emphasis being on giving generously, regularly and in keeping with our income (1 Cor. 16:2). Nevertheless, it cannot be right to conclude that the giving of God's people may be less now than it was under the law in Old Testament times.

As I intimated a moment ago, prayer and giving are closely linked. The old saying, 'Put your money where your mouth is', can be applied to mean, 'give to the cause you believe in' or 'If you are interested in a good cause, then support it financially.' Now presumably, we pray for the causes we believe in. The question is, are our prayers backed up by our giving? An old story is worth repeating. A discerning little boy said to his dad, 'Dad, if I had your chequebook, I could answer most of your prayers.'

Discipline in prayer is not easy. But it is necessary in the lives of the saints. Our pattern of prayer will vary according to our circumstances. If we have a young family, we need to pray with them. Single saints must give time to private prayer either in the morning or evening, depending on what time is best for them. Husbands and wives must also pray together. Christian husbands who find it difficult to pray with their wives should overcome their embarrassment without delay.

19. The saints' development

Do all saints make the grade?

William Farish has been called the world's most famous lazy teacher. I guess only a few people have heard of him and yet the lives of most of us are affected by his work. Farish was a tutor at Cambridge University in the late eighteenth century, and it was he who first introduced the idea of grading.

We are not sure what his motives were. Some think that because the tutors were paid according to the number of students in their classes, Farish introduced grades as a means of coping with greater numbers. The suggestion is that he was more interested in increasing his income than in getting to know his pupils. Whatever his reasons, within a few years, grades were introduced into the classroom, first in Europe and later in America.

Not everyone agrees that the use of grades has proved helpful. They argue that they prevent students from developing a keen interest in the subject being studied, their only concern being to reach the required grade and they rest content with that.

No relaxation

We can draw some interesting contrasts and comparisons with the call to holiness. Perfect likeness to Jesus Christ is the grade for which every saint should strive, even though it is unattainable in this life. He should never be content with attaining a standard that falls short of it. No matter how much progress he has made, there is always room for further improvement.

Sadly, there is a tendency among the saints – even among some older saints – to rest content when they reach a certain standard. They give the impression that there is nothing further to be achieved. The Revised Standard Version may give the impression that there are different discernable levels of holiness when it speaks of being changed into Christ's likeness from one 'degree' of glory to another (2 Cor. 3:18).

For this reason, I prefer the New International Version rendering, which says we are being transformed into his likeness with 'ever-increasing glory'. This preserves the idea of continuity to the very end of our lives. There is no suggestion of stages or grades at which we may stop learning.

No matter where we are in our Christian pilgrimage, we should never relax. Nor should our interest in the subject be allowed to wane. On the contrary, the further we go, the further we should want to go. To be content with the 'grade' we have reached and to lose interest in further development is properly called 'backsliding'.

In the last chapter, we considered the saints' fight against sin, but holiness cannot be defined merely in terms of what we try to prevent. The life of Christ revealed to us in Scripture is positive. He was always doing good and his sole aim was to do his Father's will. It follows, therefore, that as far as our spiritual development is concerned, fixing our eyes on Jesus is not only the secret of victory over sin, but also the secret of growth in wisdom and maturity.

Again, when Paul said that in Christ 'are hidden all the treasures of wisdom and knowledge' (Col. 2:3), he did not mean that we are prevented from knowing about them. As the previous verse shows, the apostle used these words because he wanted the saints in Colosse to 'be encouraged in heart and united in love, so that they may have the full riches of complete understanding'.

Indeed, he had already told them that since the day he heard about them he had not stopped praying for them, 'asking God to fill them with the knowledge of his will in all spiritual wisdom and understanding' (Col 1:9). The full riches of complete understanding have nothing to do with worldly wisdom. They come to us through the illumination of the Spirit and the Word as we grow in grace.

The purpose of these riches is to promote the spiritual development and godliness of the saints. It includes an ever-increasing ability to assess and deal with spiritual problems in ourselves and others and also, of course, a broader and deeper knowledge of the plan and purpose of God in creation and redemption. Inevitably, this leads to a deeper appreciation of what God has done for us.

In chapter 14 we thought of God as the divine lapidary. In that chapter, I explained that the best shape of a diamond is called the 'Brilliant Cut'. I did not explain that there are variations of colour in diamonds, the 'blue-white' being considered the finest. Nor did I explain that there are also variations in clarity. Some stones have obvious carbon marks and 'cracks' of one kind or another. The clearer the stone, the more precious it is.

Because I spent ten years of my life in the jewellery trade, I find myself thinking of the ability of a flawless, blue-white, brilliant cut diamond to reflect the beauty of the light as representing the perfect life of Christ. We see the reflected light in all its beauty. The carbon marks, inclusions and poor colour in an imperfect stone I see as the saint's sins and limitations; blemishes that mar the reflected beauty.

My illustration breaks down because, alas, nothing can be done about the blemishes in a diamond. They are permanent. But something can certainly be done about removing the blemishes from our lives. Indeed, with the help of the Spirit, those stubborn habits and secret sins need never be permanent. As we saw earlier, our sinful nature is always with us, but that does not mean that we should conclude that whatever prevents the beauty of Jesus being seen in us is impossible to remove.

Some Biblical examples

Seemingly, the apostle Paul had a tendency to pride! 'To keep me from becoming conceited' he confesses, 'because of these surpassingly great revelations, there was given me a thorn in my flesh, a messenger of Satan to torment me. Three times I pleaded with the Lord to take it away from me. But he said to me, "My grace is sufficient for you, for my power is made perfect in weakness."' (2 Cor. 12:7-9). Of course, the conceit that his suffering prevented would have been sinful, which means that the apostle's growth in holiness took a significant step forward when the Lord said 'No!' It was a painful way of removing a stubborn failing but better the pain than the sin.

We do not know what the thorn was, but that does not matter. Indeed, it is perhaps better not to know, because it can be thought of as any form of trial or suffering. The important factor is this – even although it was a 'messenger of Satan', it was used by the divine lapidary, not only to polish out the tendency to arrogance, but also to teach him humility. What a privilege!

That the lesson was well learned is clear from his words: 'Therefore I will boast all the more gladly about my weaknesses, so that Christ's power may rest on me. That is why, for Christ's sake, I delight in weakness, in insults, in hardships, in persecution, in difficulties. For when I am weak, then I am strong' (2 Cor. 12:9-10).

Joseph too learned wisdom from his suffering. The fact that he was dad's favourite and a spoilt child, caused his brothers to despise him. They treated him in the most appalling manner, first planning to kill him and then changing their minds and selling him to some Midianite merchants who, in turn sold him to Potiphar, one of Pharaoh's officials in Egypt.

This ill-treatment, together with the 'misfortunes' that befell him in Egypt removed the ugly blemishes from his character. Clearly, he learned wisdom from what he suffered and was able to discern God's purpose in it all.

The Psalmist tells us that they bruised Joseph's feet with shackles and put his neck in irons 'till the word of the LORD proved him true' (Ps. 105:19). Again, the divine lapidary was working on Joseph, enabling him to see that all the terrible things that happened to him had a purpose.

The generosity of his forgiving attitude to his own brothers was a moving verification of his spiritual development. Joseph was now the Prime Minister of Egypt and his brothers, who had treated him so badly, were fearful because they had discovered who he was. Would Joseph now take revenge on his brothers? Would he use his authority to punish them? Not at all. 'Do not be distressed' Joseph told them, 'and do not be angry with yourselves for selling me here, because it was to save lives that God sent me ahead of you … to preserve for you a remnant on earth and to save your lives by a great deliverance' (Gen. 45:5,7). Who would dare to say that Joseph would have achieved such a high level of faith and wisdom without his sufferings?

Jacob was a schemer and a shrewd businessman. No doubt he owed this to his mother to some extent. It was her idea to cheat Esau of his Father's blessing (Gen. 27). Jacob thought nothing of enriching himself by taking advantage of his uncle Laban. But the divine lapidary determined to knock this self-sufficiency out of his servant and teach him wisdom. He must be made to realise his dependence on his God.

Next, we see Jacob running away from Laban and returning home. He became very fearful about meeting his brother Esau and made very cunning plans to send gifts on ahead in the hope of appeasement. One night, a 'man' wrestled with Jacob and when the mysterious person saw that he could not overpower him, 'he touched the socket of Jacob's hip so that his hip was wrenched'. Jacob called the place Peniel (meaning 'the face of God') (Gen. 32:22-32).

For the rest of his life Jacob walked with a limp – a constant reminder to him of his utter dependence on God. How much better for him to be crippled than to go on living by his wits! His development as a man of God was far more important than his physical ability.

We see a similar development in every character in the Bible whom God called. No two are alike, but the purpose is exactly the same. God used the elements – the violent storm and the blazing sun – to deal with Jonah's flagrant disobedience and lack of compassion (Jonah 1 and 4). Peter's impetuosity and self-confidence received a fatal blow when his promise never to forsake his Lord was so dramatically broken (Mark:14:31, 66-72). What more can we say about Moses, Abraham, Job, all the prophets and many more?

Higher and further than you think!

After climbing a mountain for some time, the sight of a peak appears towering above us. 'Ah! That must be the top,' we say to each other. So we redouble our efforts. However, when we reach the top another, higher, peak comes into view. And when we reach the second peak, yet another appears. The mountain is much higher than we thought.

We have the same experience in our striving after holiness. I speak as one who has had seventy years' experience. Whatever height we reach, there are always greater heights to climb. 'Not that I have already obtained all this,' says Paul, 'or have already been made perfect, but I press on to take hold of that for which

Christ Jesus took hold of me … I press on toward the goal to win the prize for which God has called me heavenward in Christ Jesus' (Phil. 3:12,14).

These verses are an excellent example of the apostle's ability to assess himself. There is no arrogance here, no false claims, just a frank admission that he still has a long way to go. But there is a single-minded zeal and a determination to forget the past, with all its discouragements, successes and failures, and to strain every muscle to forge ahead.

Perhaps Paul is thinking of that 'crown of righteousness, which the Lord, the righteous Judge, will award to me on that day – and not only to me, but also to all who have longed for his appearing' (2 Tim. 4:8). He does not say what the crown is except that it is given to the righteous. James and Peter also looked forward to being crowned! James tells us that those who persevere under trial 'will receive the crown of life that God has promised to those who love him' (James 1:12). Peter says it is the faithful overseers who 'will receive the crown of glory that will never fade away' (1 Peter 5:4).

Once again, we notice in these verses an emphasis on the longing to see Jesus and the heartfelt desire to live lives pleasing to God. As we saw earlier, the longing deepens as the day draws nearer, providing we 'never tire of doing what is right' (2 Thess. 3:13).

Some readers will be aware of that pernicious doctrine that all we have to do is to stop striving and let God do it all! I look in vain to find any Scripture support for this notion. True, Jesus taught us to rest in him: 'Come to me, all you who are weary and burdened, and I will give you rest' (Matt. 11:28) but Jesus is saying that to serve him is not hard labour but joyful release. It is a serious mistake to interpret this to mean that we need not strive after holiness. Failure to do so will deprive us of that contentment that comes with godliness (1. Tim. 6:6).

Nor should we think in terms of quick-fixes. This attitude to spiritual progress has created all sorts of problems. In my youth

I, and several of my Christian friends, were led astray by the doctrine of instant sanctification. We accepted the teaching without seriously studying the Scriptures (always a very dangerous thing to do) only to discover that sin was still very much alive in us. At least, we were eager to be holy! The quick-fixes of today's church seem to offer nothing more than a 'feel-good' experience that needs to be 'topped up' every now and again.

Like the society we live in, many believers have become impatient and cannot cope with the idea of lifelong development in holiness. Whatever it is, they want it, and they want it now. And when they get it, they soon tire of it and go for the next 'blessing' that comes along. It is like trying to keep up with the latest fashion.

If only we would come back to the Scriptures, we would see that the Christian life is a lifelong battle. Our experience is God's school and he teaches every one of his pupils singly. We would also discover deep-seated exhilaration as we begin to discover what spiritual blessings really are and what purpose they serve.

What greater blessing can there be for example, than the one for which the Psalmist prayed? 'Give me understanding, and I will keep your law and obey it with all my heart. Direct me in the path of your commands, for there I find delight. Turn my heart towards your statutes and not towards selfish gain' (Ps. 119:34-36).

We insist therefore, that to test the value of any 'blessing' we need to ask how much permanent benefit it brings in our walk with God. Blessings from above do not fizzle out. What more permanent benefit can there be than a steady improvement in our likeness to our Lord Jesus? How many of us patiently seek this blessing today?

Every saint has received the gift of the Spirit, (for those who do not have the Spirit of Christ do not belong to him, Rom. 8:9). And every saint has the privilege of asking God to increase the supply of grace. Yes, the going will be tough, but there is nothing more rewarding, nothing more thrilling, than to be progressively re-created in the image of our precious Saviour, Jesus Christ.

20. The saints' trials

Are saints immune from temptation?

The matter of Uriah the Hittite

Earlier we referred briefly to King David of Israel's most appalling sin. Let us now see how it happened. One day, when his troops were fighting the enemy, he was not with them. From his vantage point, as he strolled on the palace roof in the evening, he saw a beautiful woman bathing. Her name was Bathsheba. Immediately, he was sorely tempted by lust and sent messengers to get her. She came to the palace and David, knowing she was another man's wife, slept with her.

If David had been with his troops instead of walking idly on the palace roof, this would not have happened. In the event, lust clouded his judgment, and the godly king became an adulterer. He abused his authority, taking advantage of a woman whose husband was in the army fighting the king's enemies.

Notice how things went from bad to worse. When Bathsheba informed David that she was pregnant, the king, having started the ball rolling, could not stop it. Forgetting completely whose servant he was, he sent for Uriah, Bathsheba's husband, under the pretence of wanting an update on the progress of the war, and then sent him home to his wife with a gift to follow.

The king's attempt to father the expected child on Uriah failed completely. Uriah did not go home. In the national emergency, with his colleagues dying on the battlefield, he did not think it right to enjoy the comforts of home. He slept at the entrance of the palace instead.

Not having the sense to see that his evil plans were being frustrated, David invited Uriah to the palace and made him drunk. This didn't work either. Uriah slept on his mat with the servants. The king was now on a roller coaster. In an act of reckless stupidity, he sent Uriah back to the battlefield with a letter. It contained sealed orders to Joab, the king's Commander-in-Chief, to put Uriah in the front line and then retreat, so that the innocent soldier would be exposed to enemy fire. Joab did as he was told, and Uriah died (2 Samuel 11). The Scripture tersely says: 'But the thing David had done displeased the LORD' (2 Sam. 11:27).

Those who do not have any insight into the terrible potential of the sinful nature will find the story incredible. Surely, it is not possible, they will say, for a man of God to stoop to adultery, intrigue and murder. But that is exactly what happened. The Bible summarises David's entire life in these words: 'David had done what was right in the eyes of the LORD and had not failed to keep any of the LORD's commands all the days of his life' and then, the tragic postscript is added ' – except in the case of Uriah the Hittite' (1 Kings 15:5).

Many are the lessons of this sad account. First, it gives us some tips on how to prevent a 'case of Uriah' happening in our lives. To say that if we had been in David's position, we would not have been capable of doing what he did, reveals both ignorance and arrogance. The fact of the matter is, we do fall under temptation and, at times, it can be very severe. There are also times when our hearts do not incline to obedience as much as they should. What's more, these two experiences can, and do happen at the same time, so that we become vulnerable.

What are the tips then? The most serious mistake David made, was the first one – allowing himself to remain in a situation in which he was severely tempted. There was still a way out but, once tempted, the king found it increasingly difficult to curb this illicit use of his power. He allowed himself to contemplate the forbidden pleasure. This was mistake number two. This led him to mistake number three – to turn his thoughts into action. He found out who the female was and then he sent for her. The further he went, the harder it became to stop the ball rolling.

No doubt, the king enjoyed his encounter with Bathsheba. But, as with all the pleasures of sin, the enjoyment soon turned to misery and regret. When the courageous prophet Nathan came to tell the king that God was not pleased and that the king would be severely punished, David was in agony. The God he had served so faithfully was not pleased with him.

As a child of God, the king knew that God had forgiven his sins, and yet in spite of this, David found no peace. The Lord struck Bathsheba's newly born child down and he became seriously ill. Although the king fasted and pleaded with God for the child, even lying on the floor night after night, God refused to listen. On the seventh day, the child died (2 Sam. 12:1-23).

The lesson is vital for all believers. Once, when we were unconverted, we thoroughly enjoyed our sins. But now, our loving God will not allow that to happen any more. Moreover, we should let it sink deep into our hearts that although God has promised to forgive all our sins, past, present and future, there is a price we must pay in this life. The painful consequences of David's sin followed him for the rest of his life, and so will ours.

Temptation and godly habits

'No one has ever suffered temptation like this.' This is the sort of thing we may want to say to ourselves when we are going through a severe trial. Thinking along these lines, however, is a mistake that makes us more likely to give way. In fact, we are blaming God because we feel that he has allowed the temptation to become too severe – something he has promised not to do. We persuade ourselves that we are to be excused because ours is a special case!

In 1 Corinthians 10:13, along with the promise, comes the clear assertion that temptation is common in the lives of the saints: 'No temptation has seized you except what is common to man. And God is faithful; he will not let you be tempted beyond what you can bear.' Peter too makes the same point: 'Dear friends, do not be surprised at the painful trial you are suffering, as though something strange were happening to you' (1 Peter 4:12). 'Resist him [the Devil], standing firm in the faith, because you know that your brothers throughout the world are undergoing the same kind of sufferings' (1 Peter 5:9).

This robs me of my excuses. My temptation is not special. Indeed, it is quite general. My fellow believers all over the world are coping with it in its various forms. And since God has promised to keep temptation within my ability to resist, if I give way to it, I am to blame and no one else.

When we are facing severe temptations, habits formed over the years will come to our aid. Indeed, whether we are suffering temptation or opposition – anything that causes us to feel vulnerable and exposed – an established routine will prove to be a great blessing. In these circumstances, there is nothing hypocritical about sticking to a routine of Bible-reading, prayer and worship, even if we do not feel inclined. Satan's intention is to break down the good habits we have formed.

Believers who lack discipline in their daily routine when times are easier, are much more likely to be blown off course when the going gets tough. As the writer to the Hebrews says: 'We want each of you to show this same diligence to the very end, in order to make your hope sure. We do not want you to become lazy, but to imitate those who through faith and patience inherit what has been promised' (Heb. 6:11-12).

But I must not give the impression that resisting temptation is just a matter of going through a routine of religious duties. We are talking here about the benefit of established godly habits and only godly people are able to form them. If, for example, it is my settled habit to read the Word and pray at a certain time during the day it will, under normal circumstances, be a time of joy. To allow the temptation to abandon that routine would be folly in the extreme.

Going through an established routine in using the means of grace is never boring for those who really appreciate what God has done for them. In any case, failure to establish a routine is highly likely to lead to slackness and neglect. It is folly to assume that growth in personal holiness just happens.

21. The saints' limitations

Do saints ever achieve perfection?

Perfectionism

Recently I was papering a ceiling. Those who have done it will know that it is not easy when standing on the top of a ladder trying to get the paper edge to edge. I succeeded in getting it right until the last piece. By that time, my neck was protesting. Now, every time I look up at the ceiling I feel frustrated because there is a slight overlap in one place. Now if you describe me as a perfectionist, I am not going to argue. The fact is, I am never completely satisfied with what I do, whether it is papering ceilings, painting pictures or preaching the gospel.

According to the analysts, perfectionism creates tension, not only for the sufferer but also for the people he works with. For one thing, it undermines the confidence of others because they are made to feel they cannot be trusted to do the job properly. The perfectionist suffers if he is persuaded to delegate the work to others because he lives in fear that they will make a mess of it.

It is a time waster too. The point is reached where the extra time spent in trying to achieve that elusive high standard could be better spent doing other things. It is like the law of diminishing returns. As more time is put in, less and less is achieved. I have read somewhere that this can lead to all kinds of mental disorder, so I had better be careful!

But there is another kind of perfectionism. Some Christians believe they can attain it in this life. And worse, unbelievably, there are some who think they have actually attained it! Thankfully, there are not so many of them around as there used to be when I was younger. If it were not so sad, it would be highly amusing because those who make the claim are the only ones who see themselves as sinless. Others can see their blemishes a mile away, even without their spectacles. The arrogance of the claim is astounding.

I have a double purpose in writing this chapter. First I want to give a warning to those who are in danger of being persuaded that they can attain perfection in this life. Thankfully, most believers are realistic enough to admit how far from it they are. Second, I want to give some encouragement to those saints who get rather downhearted because they think they are not making much progress at all.

To believe in the possibility of sinless perfection betrays a serious lack of understanding, particularly about the nature of sin. Therefore, those in the first group should spend more time studying the holiness of God and the depravity of the human heart. John tells us that 'if we claim to be without sin, we deceive ourselves and the truth is not in us' (1 John 1:8). To say the least, for perfectionists to quarrel with the apostle is an unreasonable attitude to adopt.

Not only is perfectionism contrary to Scripture, it is contrary to experience as well. Since 'everything that does not come from faith is sin' (Rom 14:23), who is free of guilt? 'If it does not come from faith' means 'if we are not sure that God would approve'. Remember too, that according to Jesus, a man who looks lustfully at a woman is guilty of adultery. And he who is angry with his brother is guilty of murder (Matt. 5:22,28).

When the Psalmist posed the question, 'If you, O LORD, kept a record of sins, O Lord, who could stand?', he did not stop to answer it because the answer is so obvious. This is why he immediately goes on to talk about God's forgiveness (Ps. 130:3-4). The believer who claims to be sinless is fooling no one but himself. The sooner he changes his mind the sooner he will start making progress in holiness. Until this happens, he is in danger of making a fool of himself and his sanctification is on hold.

Those in the opposite camp need encouragement. Many saints are deeply shocked by the state of their own hearts. Of course, it is only since they believed that they have felt like this. One woman stands out in my memory. After she had been a Christian for a short time, she came to me in distress and said something along these lines: 'I can't be a true believer; I am horrified by what goes through my mind.'

For a moment, she seemed even more horrified when I told her that this was a sign of progress. I explained to her that before they are born anew, sinners are not usually bothered about their sins. Most insist most strenuously that they are as good as anyone else. (If I were given a hundred pounds for every time someone claimed to me to be good, I would be a wealthy man!)

But when people turn to Christ, I explained, they begin to see their sins as God sees them and it is not a pretty sight. Knowing the true state of our hearts is essential if we are to make progress in the Christian life. It was so obvious to me that the troubled woman was growing in grace rapidly but was unaware of it. At the age of 86, I am still saying 'God be merciful to me, a sinner' and with more feeling than ever.

'So I find this law at work' says Paul, 'When I want to do good, evil is right there with me. For in my inner being I delight in God's law; but I see another law at work in the members of my body, waging war against the law of my mind and making me a prisoner of the law of sin at work within my members' (Rom. 7:21-23). Any lack of frankness and honesty in this matter forms no part of saintliness.

Over the years I have also known several Christian believers who have been troubled by the words of Jesus recorded in Matthew 5:48: 'Be perfect, therefore, as your heavenly Father is perfect.' They reason like this: since I am very conscious of my sins I cannot be making much progress in the Christian life because the standard Jesus expects is perfection.

Now, just in case the reader is grappling with this problem, here is a little Greek lesson that will help you. The Greek word *teleios*, translated 'perfect' in the above text, has different shades of meaning. Take Hebrews 5:14 for example, where the writer tells us that solid food is for the 'mature'. This is also *teleios*. Or take Philippians 3:12, where the apostle Paul, after addressing the subject of striving after likeness to Jesus, admits that he has not 'already been made perfect'. The word 'perfect' here is *teleioo* (pronounced tel-i-o'-o) which is in the same family as *teleios*, but means accomplished or finished. Then he adds: 'All of us who are mature (*teleios* again) should take such a view of things' (Phil 3:15).

Now it would be utterly ridiculous to say that all of us who are perfect should admit that we are not yet perfect. Therefore, we can be confident that Jesus is not demanding sinless perfection of his disciples. As we saw earlier, the fight against sin in our lives will go on relentlessly until the day we die. Only then shall we be able to say we have finished the race.

When Paul cried out, 'What a wretched man I am! Who will rescue me from this body of death?' he answered his own question: 'Thanks be to God – through Jesus Christ our Lord' (Rom. 7:24-25). But this does not mean, as some suppose, that the Lord Jesus Christ will deliver us from the struggle in this life. No! The apostle is eagerly longing for the deliverance that will be his when the Lord returns and he receives a new and perfect body, no longer subject to sin. This is clear if we complete the text: 'So then, I myself in my mind am a slave to God's law, but in the sinful nature a slave to the law of sin.'

Self-assessment

After nearly forty years, I am still in touch with the woman I mentioned earlier. During those years, she has made excellent progress but has not changed her opinion of herself. Nor should she. When Paul was old, he too still regarded himself as the worst of sinners (1 Tim. 1:15).

Why, you may ask? There are several reasons. First, our ability to make a true assessment of ourselves in the sight of God grows as we grow in saintliness. That is to say, the more progress we make on the path of holiness, the keener our awareness of the nature and extent of sin in the human heart becomes. This give rise to a paradox – the more holy we become, the more conscious we are of our sins.

Second, as we become more mature, sins come to light that we did not know about. For example, when I was first converted, I felt free from the sin of hypocrisy. I despised the Pharisees for their play-acting (the word 'hypocrite' originally meant an actor). But now I understand that to put on a front in a feeble attempt to make myself appear to be better than I am, is hypocrisy. How many of us, I wonder, behave as carefully at home with our wives or husbands and families, as we do in the office, the workshop, or the church fellowship. Acting a part in order to impress others is the sin that made Jesus angry.

Third, for the saints to make claims about themselves is unseemly. Anyone who does so merely advertises his arrogance and his inability to assess himself. It is for others to see our good deeds and praise our Father in heaven (Matt. 5:16).

Finally, the more we become conscious of our sinful nature and its potential, the more we are assured that the sinlessness of Christ is reckoned as ours. If we turn this around it will still be true – the more we are assured that God reckons Christ's righteousness as ours, the more we become conscious of our sins.

For this reason, it is no longer possible for the maturing saint to think that personal holiness earns or contributes to his salvation. The striving after holiness has altogether different motives. We are increasingly grateful to God for our great salvation and we want to be more like Jesus day by day as we prepare to meet him.

Apart, then, from the Lord Jesus Christ, the perfect man does not exist. He alone among men was without sin. He challenged the Jews who would not believe his words, 'Can any of you prove me guilty of sin?' (John 8:46). Neither they, nor anyone else could do it.

Part Four

The saints' destiny

22. The saints' judgment

Will the saints be called to account?

An affirmative answer to our opening question may come as a shock to some readers. They rejoice, quite rightly, in the blessedness of 'the man whose sin the Lord will never count against him' (Rom. 4:8) but make the serious and erroneous assumption that they no longer have a moral obligation to keep the law.

Comparing Scripture with Scripture

To come to a biblically sound conclusion on this matter, it is essential, as always, to go first to the classic statement of the doctrine. It is foolish in the extreme to base our doctrine on isolated or ambiguous texts which may seem to say something different. It is also vital that we keep texts in their contexts. A superficial knowledge of the Scriptures can be dangerous. Or, to put it another way, knowing texts out of their context can be misleading. No matter what subject we study, comparing Scripture with Scripture is vital.

To give a crude but obvious example, we hear people say 'money is the root of all evil', believing it to be the teaching of the Bible. The words are based on 1 Timothy 6:10 which states, 'For the love of money is a root of all kinds of evil'. There's nothing wrong with money; the love of money is the problem.

Again, critics of the Bible seize on the apparent contradictions. But when we understand the context of the passages in question, we see that the 'contradiction' is more apparent than real. For example, the apostle Paul tells us in Galatians 6:2 that we should 'carry each other's burdens'. Yet, in the next breath, he says that each of us 'should carry his own load' (Gal. 6:5). How easy it would be to jump to the conclusion that Paul has contradicted himself.

As we saw in chapter 8, our first response to those who would immediately assume that the apostle is at fault would be to insist that he is not stupid. Why should we expect a man of his calibre to contradict himself? We would not criticise a respected and intelligent friend in this way, so why do it to Paul? Knowing, therefore, what sort of man he was, we conclude that there must be a reasonable explanation for the apparent contradiction. In the above example, it should be clear to any careful reader that, if they can be shared, no one should be left to bear his burdens alone. 'A burden shared is a burden halved' we say. By bearing our burdens the Lord Jesus left an example for us to follow (1 Pet. 5:7). This is what Paul means in the first quotation.

But if we are too proud to help our burdened brother because we just don't want to be bothered with his problems, we are guilty of sin in the sight of God. We alone will have to bear our load of guilt for such behaviour because, on the Day of Judgment, it cannot be shared with anyone else. This is what Paul means in the second quotation.

Here are two more quotations relating to the matter of judgment that are apparently contradictory. Paul says: 'You, then, why do you judge your brother? Or why do you look down on your brother? For we will all stand before God's judgment seat' (Rom. 14:10). Yet, Jesus said: 'Verily, I say unto you, He that heareth my word, and believeth him that sent me, hath eternal life, and cometh not into judgment, but hath passed out of death into life' (John 5:24, American Standard Version).

How can we explain this? Paul insists that we will all be judged, but Jesus says believers will not be judged! Again, the answer is not difficult. In some older translations, like the ASV quotation above, the word 'judgment' means 'the judgment of condemnation'. Believers cannot be condemned because they have already 'crossed over from death to life'. The newer versions make this clear.

My third example on the same subject is, perhaps, the most difficult of all and it demonstrates the importance of keeping texts in their context. Indeed, failure to apply this principle will almost certainly lead us astray here. After exposing the true nature of the human heart, the apostle Paul concludes: 'Therefore no-one will be declared righteous in his [God's] sight by observing the law; rather, through the law we become conscious of sin' (Rom. 3:20). In harmony with this, in his letter to the Ephesians he says: 'For it is by grace you have been saved, through faith – and this not from yourselves, it is the gift of God – not by works, so that no-one can boast' (Eph. 2:8-9).

Yet, speaking of 'the day of God's wrath, when his righteous judgment will be revealed' the same apostle says: 'God "will give to each person according to what he has done". To those who by persistence in doing good seek glory, honour and immortality, he will give eternal life. But for those who are self-seeking and who reject the truth and follow evil, there will be wrath and anger' (Rom. 2:5-8). How can we be saved by grace *and* by our good deeds? They are mutually exclusive.

How then do we reconcile these apparently conflicting statements? First of all, let us ask ourselves a simple question. How would God's justice be vindicated if, on the Day of Judgment he publicly declared openly wicked people 'not guilty' just because they professed to be Christians?

The words of Jesus are relevant and clear: 'Not everyone who says to me, "Lord, Lord," will enter the kingdom of heaven, but only he who does the will of my Father who is in heaven. Many will say to me on that day, "Lord, Lord, did we not prophesy in your name, and in your name drive out demons and perform many miracles?" Then I will tell them plainly, "I never knew you. Away from me, you evildoers!"' (Matt. 7:21-23).

The Lord Jesus is telling us that only those who do the will of God will enter heaven. He is also warning us against the possibility of being an evildoer who is in the habit of calling him 'Lord' and performing miracles in his name! A holy life is the only qualification we need to enter heaven. Using the right language and working miracles are no substitute.

Now hear Paul on the subject: 'For we must all appear before the judgment seat of Christ, that each one may receive what is due to him for the things done while in the body, whether good or bad' (2 Cor. 5:10). Nothing could be clearer than this.

As we saw earlier, the only exception to this is when a true believer dies soon after his conversion to Christ and, like the dying thief, is deprived of the opportunity to grow in holiness. The Judge of all the earth knows whether his profession is sincere or not. If it is, the verdict will be 'not guilty', because we are saved by grace.

So, in common with everyone else in the world, our eternal destiny is either heaven or hell. Heaven is presented to us in the Scriptures, first as a free gift of divine grace and second, as a reward of grace for faithful service. It can never be seen as something we earn. Hell, on the other hand, will be the place where God's just punishment of all those who do not trust in Christ alone for salvation will be carried out. They will be condemned for failing to keep God's law.

The nature of rewards

It is said that 'virtue is its own reward' but I guess most people think of rewards in terms of money offered for things like the recovery of lost property, or for information leading to the arrest of a criminal. In other words, they think of a reward as something earned by being public spirited or by doing something beyond the call of duty.

Usually, people are not inclined to be whistleblowers (informers), even when serious crime is involved. Apparently, however, this attitude changes dramatically if a sufficient cash reward is offered. The American government spends vast sums of money in rewarding citizens who give information leading to the recovery of money obtained by fraud. Thirty per cent of the sum recovered is given to the whistleblower. According to reports, some payments have been in excess of a hundred million dollars.

When we come to the meaning of the word 'reward' in the Scriptures however, we have to jettison these ideas. God is no man's debtor. His rewards are not of debt but of grace. The main idea is that salvation in itself is the greatest reward, but the word carries different meanings in different contexts. The Master's words make it clear that the reward cannot be for merit: 'So you also, when you have done everything you were told to do, should say, "We are unworthy servants; we have only done our duty"' (Luke 17:10).

In Psalm 19:11 we have a slightly different meaning. When the Psalmist speaks of rewards for obedience, he is thinking of the immediate benefits. Speaking of God's commands, he says: 'in keeping them there is great reward'. The little word 'in' tells us that the reward is the joy and freedom of obedience that is ours here and now.

Scripture does not say much about the nature of those rewards that are a bonus for the faithful. The apostle Paul speaks of one: 'For what is our hope, our joy, or the crown in which we will glory in the presence of our Lord Jesus when he comes? Is it not you? Indeed, you are our glory and joy' (1 Thess. 2:19-20).

The words of Jesus recorded in Matthew 25:23 also suggest another. The faithful servant will be blessed with greater responsibility: 'Well done, good and faithful servant! You have been faithful with a few things; I will put you in charge of many things. Come and share your master's happiness!'

Jesus also speaks of future rewards for his disciples in Matthew 5:12. Pronouncing them 'blessed' when they are persecuted, he says: 'Rejoice and be glad, because great is your reward in heaven.' The meaning here seems to be that those who suffer for Christ will never be the ultimate losers.

The future rewards God offers for obedience apply only to genuine believers. And we must always be careful to distinguish between believers who lose their reward (by neglecting the means of grace), and unbelievers who suffer eternal loss (by ignoring the offer of a great salvation (Heb. 2:3)). The reward is everlasting happiness (blessedness) for the believer and the punishment is eternal destruction for the unbeliever. Confusion at this point is destructive and will undermine our assurance of eternal life.

Jesus highlights the terrible alternatives in his account of the separation of the sheep and the goats: 'When the Son of Man comes in his glory, and all the angels with him, he will sit on his throne in heavenly glory. All the nations will be gathered before him, and he will separate the people one from another as a shepherd separates the sheep from the goats' (Matt. 25:31-32).

In the light of this, we can afford to leave those who persecute us in God's hands because 'God is just: He will pay back trouble to those who trouble you ... This will happen when the Lord Jesus is revealed from heaven in blazing fire with his powerful angels' (2 Thess. 1:6,7).

Again, it must be emphasised that the rewards are related to deeds and not merely to professions of faith. And not only to our deeds, but also to the motive for our deeds. God 'will bring to light what is hidden in darkness and will expose the motives of men's hearts. At that time each will receive his praise from God' (1 Cor. 4:5). 'Behold, I am coming soon! My reward is with me, and I will give to everyone according to what he has done' (Rev. 22:12).

Before leaving this subject, we should be clear in our minds that God's 'divine power has given us everything we need for life and godliness through our knowledge of him who called us by his own glory and goodness' (2 Peter 1:3). Therefore we are blameworthy if we do not take full advantage of God's provision.

Paul found it necessary to rebuke the believers in Corinth because they were not making any progress. He insists that no other foundation can be laid other than Jesus Christ and warns them to be careful how they build upon it. 'If any man builds on this foundation using gold, silver, costly stones, wood, hay or straw, his work will be shown for what it is, because the Day will bring it to light. It will be revealed with fire, and the fire will test the quality of each man's work. If what he has built survives, he will receive his reward. If it is burned up, he will suffer loss; he himself will be saved, but only as one escaping through the flames' (1 Cor. 3:12-15).

To miss a God-given opportunity to live our lives for the glory of God and to scrape into heaven by a whisker must be better than being excluded altogether. But what a wasted life! How much better to 'receive a rich welcome into the eternal kingdom of our Lord and Saviour Jesus Christ' (2 Peter 1:11).

Conclusion

So we come back to where we started, but hopefully a little wiser. There is only one way to heaven. From a human point of view it is the way of repentance and faith in Jesus Christ. From God's point of view it is the way of justification by faith leading to holiness. Justified persons are the only ones who 'by persistence in doing good seek glory, honour and immortality'. The alternative is too terrible to think about.

But the call to holiness is not a demand for perfection in this life. Perfection must wait for heaven. The shortcomings of holy people are many and varied. But neither is this a reason for slackness. Every effort must be made, as we saw in chapter 15 when we discussed the saints' responsibility, to add goodness, knowledge, self-control, perseverance, godliness, brotherly kindness and love to our faith (2 Peter 1:5-7).

23. The saints' resurrection

In what kind of body do the saints come?

The purpose of our sanctification

Why do colleges and universities exist? Is it so that the students can have a good time and enjoy the experience of learning? I have no doubt that many who go thoroughly enjoy it, but if that were the only reason, it would be a sad case of selfish indulgence.

The purpose of the exercise is to gain a qualification in some specialised field so that the student may become an engineer, an architect, a doctor, physician, mathematician and so forth. He should then be in a position to earn a good living and contribute something to society. The training is a means to an end.

Similarly, in the school of life, the saints are being trained for a purpose. Growth in sanctification is not an end in itself although, contrary to popular belief, there is great joy in holy living. Rather, it is a necessary preparation for the glory of heaven.

Careful study of the Scriptures will show that the Christian gospel is forward looking. This is because the best is yet future. We have been redeemed in order that we may glorify God for ever. It is a serious mistake, therefore, to think only in terms of the blessings we receive from him, great as they are. True, without him we can do nothing, but the help of the Holy Spirit is with a view to enabling us to serve the Lord in such a way that God is glorified in our lives here and now, in this world. This training, which is with a view to sharing 'in the inheritance of the saints in the kingdom of light' (Col. 1:12) demands effort and dedication.

But, unlike the student whose final examinations are set for a certain time, God has already qualified us because of what Christ has done for us. That is to say, if we should die prematurely, we are not disadvantaged in any way. For at whatever time our lives end in this world, the qualification is ours. The entire process of our sanctification therefore, however long or short it is, must be seen as a preparation for the sharing of the glory of Christ.

Of course, the time of the end of our lives in this world is not left to chance. God himself has already fixed it. Until that day arrives, we cannot enjoy the actual benefits of the glory to come. As several writers have said, the blessings of the Christian life are both 'now' and 'not yet'. The joys of the 'not yet' for which we must wait, far exceed those of the 'now'. For example, the promise of no more tears, no more death, mourning, crying or pain must wait for the new heaven and new earth (Rev. 21:1-4).

We know that the 'the Lord himself will come down from heaven, with a loud command, with the voice of the archangel and with the trumpet call of God and the dead in Christ will rise first. After that, we who are still alive and are left will be caught up together with them in the clouds to meet the Lord in the air. And so we will be with the Lord for ever' (1 Thess. 4:16-17).

Speculation about the date of Christ's coming is fruitless. The angels do not know and not even Jesus himself knew (Matt. 24:36). Paul's purpose in writing the above was not to excite the curiosity of the Thessalonians but to reassure them that those saints who have died will not be missing on the great day. Indeed, none of the prophecies of his coming is written to encourage speculation. They are intended to warn and encourage believers.

The resurrection body

Paul's reference to the 'trumpet call of God' reminds us of his classic statement about the bodily resurrection of the dead in chapter fifteen of his first letter to the Corinthians. The trumpets are mentioned at verse 52: We will not all sleep, says the apostle, but we will all be changed 'in a flash, in the twinkling of an eye, at the last trumpet. For the trumpet will sound, the dead will be raised imperishable, and we will be changed.'

Trumpets were used in ancient Israel for calling people together (Num. 10:2) and this is the idea of Paul's statement. In a split second, all the saints on earth or in heaven, will be called together, having inherited their new and perfect bodies and we shall be with the Lord for ever (1 Thess. 4:17).

In that moment, we shall realise as never before, why the scales always come down heavily on the glory side when weighed against the physical sufferings of the past. And I am persuaded that Paul included our physical sufferings when he said: 'I consider that our present sufferings are not worth comparing with the glory that will be revealed in us' (Rom. 8:18). It is certainly not always easy to see it like this, especially when the pain and suffering are severe, but the more we are able to do so, the more likely we are to benefit from it and see it as a necessity.

When I look into the mirror these days, I am not thrilled by what I see. I have reached the stage where I feel a little hard done by when the dentist charges me the full price for a check up. To examine my few remaining teeth takes him less than a minute.

And not long ago, when I was driving the car, I said to my wife, 'would you mind closing your window, the wind is blowing my hair about.' 'Which one?' she asked. She did not mean which window. My wrinkles are also much deeper than they used to be. Tiredness catches up with me long before bedtime. And my sleep is broken by frequent trips to the bathroom.

But that is not all. My old body still interferes with my godly ambitions. It prevents me from doing what I want to do (Rom. 7:18-24). The evil thoughts that originate in my mind without warning still bother me. Younger readers may be surprised at this, mistakenly thinking that the temptations of the body are no longer a trouble in old age. Don't believe it! The old body is, and always has been, the most persistent handicap in our growth in holiness.

I need no persuading that the body I am in is not fit for purpose in the new world. How ridiculous it would be to think of introducing an old decaying body, still subject to death and defilement, into a world where everything is pure and incorruptible! I am looking forward to seeing myself in a heavenly mirror if they exist! Then, I shall not be disappointed because ugliness will be a thing of the past.

'But our citizenship is in heaven', says Paul, 'And we eagerly await a Saviour from there, the Lord Jesus Christ, who, by the power that enables him to bring everything under his control, will transform our lowly bodies so that they will be like his glorious body' (Phil. 3:20-21). What a glorious prospect!

Nor is there any need to worry about not being able to recognise the people we have known and loved as fellow believers here on earth. Although my resurrection body will be totally new, it will still be my body and recognisable as such. Being glorified does not mean losing my identity. Many questions may arise in the mind of the reader at this point. For example, how will I recognise the old people I knew when they no longer look old? Such questions are futile because the answers are outside our present understanding.

The purifying hope

According to the apostle John, 'Everyone who has this hope in him purifies himself, just as he is pure' (1 John 3:3). John is not advocating some kind of do-it-yourself holiness. He is saying that having a confident expectation of seeing Jesus face to face has a powerful influence on our morals. There is, of course, a real sense in which we are to keep ourselves pure (1 Tim. 5:22), but as we saw earlier, we now co-operate with the Spirit. Our striving after holiness is given a huge boost by the knowledge that we are to see Jesus.

Sadly, many saints are slow to develop the habit of looking forward to the future glory. If they are true saints, they will not be deprived of the glory because of it, but they will not benefit from its purifying influence. If the reader is among them, he must take steps to put this right without delay. No matter what age we have reached, we still have a responsibility to strip away the clutter that mars our vision. As the writer to the Hebrews says: 'Let us throw off everything that hinders and the sin that so easily entangles, and let us run with perseverance the race marked out for us' (Heb. 12:1).

24. The saints' inheritance

What do saints look forward to?

Expectation and realization

In this life, the proverb 'expectation is better than realization' is usually true to experience. The proverb is both pessimistic and realistic and, thankfully, there are some exceptions. Even so, it is a common experience to be thrilled with the prospect of some event only to be bitterly disappointed when, or soon after, it takes place.

I remember our first visit to Spain. My expectation of beautiful views from the balcony of our comfortable accommodation was never realized. To see anything at all we had to go out on to the balcony, and from there, we only had a view of the high-rise block of flats opposite. The beds were not comfortable. Even if they had been, the deep beat of the music from a local bar would have kept us awake. It did not stop until about five in the morning, every morning. All the electric sockets in the apartment were loose and dangerous, some literally hanging off the wall. Some catering staff in the local restaurants and pubs were on strike and there was violence in the streets. How glad we were to come home.

I must not give the impression that life is a disappointment. Much depends on the realism of our expectation. If, for example, you appreciate the beauty of creation as I do, you will never be disappointed with it. The difficulty here, at least for me, is not having the ability to retain the sheer splendour of the places I have visited. I remember the scenes well enough but cannot recapture the atmosphere and magnificence of them.

Was Wordsworth, I wonder, an exception to this? The second verse of his well-known poem about the daffodils seems to claim an ability to retain the grandeur well after his visit. For those who may not be familiar with the poem, here are the first two verses:

> I wandered lonely as a cloud
> That floats on high o'er vales and hills,
> When all at once I saw a crowd,
> A host of golden daffodils;
> Beside the lake, beneath the trees,
> Fluttering and dancing in the breeze.

In the second verse, Wordsworth is no longer at the scene, and yet he is able to say:

> For oft when on my couch I lie
> In vacant or in pensive mood,
> They flash upon that inward eye
> Which is the bliss of solitude,
> And then my heart with pleasure fills,
> And dances with the daffodils.

Recapturing the scene with my 'inward eye' is not too difficult for me, but to say that my heart 'dances with the daffodils' would hardly be true. I prove this to myself when I go back again to the scene. If it were another walk along the shoreline of Windermere on a sunny spring morning when the daffodils are in full bloom, I would realise immediately that I had not retained the grandeur and the thrilling atmosphere of the scene. But now, as I see it again, my delight is renewed as the glory of the place comes back to me.

Indeed, it seems greater than anything I remember on previous visits. Evidently, Wordsworth's memory was more retentive than mine, or was he just being poetic?

What a difference I find when it comes to the glimpses Scripture provides of the Lord's coming in glory. Obviously, they cannot possibly transport us into the delight we shall experience on the occasion. And yet, there are times when the glory of it, to use Wordsworth's words, flashes upon that inward eye and causes the heart to dance with joy. In this case, although I have seen but a poor reflection of the glory to come, my ability to take delight in it increases as the years go by. I can only conclude that these thrilling and ever more delightful foretastes are the gift of the Spirit.

What is this glory?

What do we mean by 'glory'? According to the *Chambers Dictionary*, the word means several things: 'great honour and prestige, great beauty or splendour, praise and thanks given to God, a greatly-admired asset, a halo round a saint's head in a painting and the splendour and blessedness of heaven.' A simple definition of the word in the way the Bible uses it would be 'the outshining of God's excellence'. The literal meaning of the Hebrew word for 'glory' is 'weight'. The apostle Paul was almost certainly playing on this word when he told the Christians in Corinth that 'our light and momentary troubles are achieving for us an eternal glory that far outweighs them all' (2 Cor. 4:17).

But what is this outshining of God's excellence that we see in Christ? Certainly, the glory of the monarchs of this world do not compare with it. Jesus tells us that even the glory of King Solomon was surpassed by the splendour of the lilies of the field (Matt. 6:29). Nor can it be the glory of the earthly body of Jesus of Nazareth. He was so disfigured that many people were deeply shocked (Isa. 52:14). Nor, it seems, will it be that indescribable glory of God, which no man is allowed to see (Exod. 33:20).

The best way to answer this question is to ask what glory was it that the disciples saw in Jesus? Although to everyone else Jesus appeared as a man, the disciples saw beyond his earthly appearance and were able to perceive his glory. Indeed, on the Mount of Transfiguration, Peter, James and John saw the face of Jesus shining like the sun and his clothes as white as light (Matt. 17:2).

Probably with this experience in mind, the apostle John testifies: 'We have seen his glory, the glory of the one and only [Son], who came from the Father, full of grace and truth' (John 1:14). Surely then, the glory of Christ that we shall see when he comes is the same glory, except that it will be much more than a temporary glimpse. It will be the same in character but far greater in intensity and duration. When Jesus appears in glory, the fullness of his grace and truth will radiate from his Person forever. And – thanks be to God – it will also radiate from ours.

Although words are limited, our expectation is set out graphically in Scripture. As we saw just now, Paul speaks of 'the eternal weight of glory' far surpassing our momentary suffering. And, as we saw earlier, in Romans 8:18, he says: 'I consider that our present sufferings are not worth comparing with the glory that will be revealed in us.' To be glorified is a destiny so great that, by comparison, a life of suffering for Christ will seem like a brief and insignificant episode. These and many other verses greatly encourage God's suffering saints and cause their hearts to dance at the prospect.

I remember taking my family to Switzerland for the first time. For weeks, before we set out, we were studying the maps and reading about the country. By the time we arrived, we had formed a good idea of the beauty of the place. This was certainly an occasion when the realisation was better than the expectation. But it was the expectation that motivated us to find out about the place.

Even though we have never seen Jesus, he is precious to us. He, the King of kings, is our brother. He redeemed us by his precious blood. He is more to us than life itself. Can anyone wonder why we are ecstatic at the prospect of spending eternity with him? 'Now I know in part; then I shall know fully, even as I am fully known' (1 Cor. 13:12).

The new heaven and new earth

The creation is waiting for that great day too. Paul tells us that 'The creation waits in eager expectation for the sons of God to be revealed. For the creation was subjected to frustration, not by its own choice, but by the will of the one who subjected it...' This was God, of course, for he is the only one who could ensure that the subjection was not permanent. He subjected it 'in hope that the creation itself will be liberated from its bondage to decay and brought into the glorious freedom of the children of God' (Rom. 8:19-21).

Why, do you think, does creation have to wait for the sons of God to be revealed? Obviously, there would be no point in setting creation free from its bondage unless the saints were also set free from theirs. Nor would there be any reason for the saints to receive their new and perfect bodies in a world still subject to decay. The two events must occur together – new people for a new world.

Seeing Jesus by faith is what we are doing right now in this world. But in that day, faith will give way to sight. The first is as essential preparation for the second. The saints are the only people in the world who are privileged to live with such a glorious expectation. Others cannot know anything about it and would not understand it. In old age, the hope gets brighter as the days go by. Let me be clear, no one will realise it who is not expecting it. Those who do not see the glory of Christ by faith will never behold it by sight.

It is common practice among the saints to speak of believers who have died as having 'gone to heaven', or 'gone to be with the Lord'. For some, this may conjure up images of disembodied spirits drifting aimlessly and endlessly around in space. Nothing could be further from the truth. The final destination of the saints is a transformed universe. As far back as the eighth century BC, God revealed the new order to Isaiah: 'Behold, I will create new heavens and a new earth. The former things will not be remembered, nor will they come to mind' (Isa. 65:17).

The apostle Peter takes up the theme: 'The heavens will disappear with a roar; the elements will be destroyed by fire, and the earth and everything in it will be laid bare' (2 Peter 3:10). Then he adds: 'But in keeping with his promise we are looking forward to a new heaven and a new earth, the home of righteousness' (2 Peter 3:13).

The Book of Revelation gives us even more insights. In the vision God gave to the apostle John, he saw 'a new heaven and a new earth...' Then John heard a loud voice from the throne of God saying, 'Now the dwelling of God is with men, and he will live with them. They will be his people, and God himself will be with them and be their God. He will wipe every tear from their eyes. There will be no more death or mourning or crying or pain, for the old order of things has passed away' (Rev. 21:1-4). Sin, sickness and sorrow, along with everything else we suffered in this perishing body in this decaying world, will be a thing of the past. Obviously, when death is destroyed, the sin that caused it will also bite the dust.

But this 'freedom from' does not leave us in a vacuum. The saints do not only look forward to freedom *from* sickness, pain and death, but also *to* serving the Lord in a world of perfect righteousness: 'No longer will there be any curse. The throne of God and of the Lamb will be in the city, and his servants will serve him. They will see his face, and his name will be on their foreheads. There will be no more night. They will not need the light of a lamp or the light of the sun, for the Lord God will give them light. And they will reign for ever and ever' (Rev. 22:3-5).

We have the word of Jesus for it, that the glory of heaven is the inheritance of God's elect people and has been made ready since the world was made: 'Come, you who are blessed by my Father; take your inheritance, the kingdom prepared for you since the creation of the world' (Matt. 25:34).

In summary, we shall have a new world and a new body to enjoy it. Our feet will be planted firmly on the ground, and we shall live forever. We shall serve the Lord with great joy, for Christ the King will make 'us to be a kingdom and priests to serve his God and Father' (Rev. 1:6). It is a sure and certain hope, depending on God's promises. This, and nothing less, is the inheritance of the saints.

'Having believed, you were marked in him with a seal, the promised Holy Spirit, who is a deposit guaranteeing our inheritance until the redemption of those who are God's possession – to the praise of his glory' (Eph. 1:13-14).

Gloria in Excelsis Deo

Appendix:
The saints' life after death

Will the saints go to sleep?

Soul sleep

I never get an unbroken sleep these nights. When the interruptions are frequent, my mind sometimes goes back to childhood when, after being put to bed, the next thing I knew, it was time to get up.

For centuries, many in the church have believed the teaching that after death the souls of the saints are in unconscious repose. This has been called 'soul sleep'. Some are not unduly troubled by it because, like my childhood sleep, the darkness of the night passes without knowing anything about it. But is this what Scripture teaches?

The idea is based on the frequent references to death as sleep in the New Testament. In 1 Cor. 15:6, Paul tells us that Jesus appeared after his resurrection to 'more than five hundred of the brothers at the same time, most of whom are still living, though some have fallen asleep'. Jesus too, told those who were mourning the death of Jairus's daughter that she was not dead, but asleep (Matt. 9:24).

Others, including myself, take the view that this kind of language is adopted, not to teach that after death the believing soul is asleep, but to make the point that for the saints, death has been robbed of its terrors.

Not having the benefit of the fuller revelations of the New Testament, the Old Testament writers do not shed much light on the problem. 'No-one remembers you when he is dead. Who praises you from his grave?' (Ps. 6:5) is sometimes taken mistakenly to mean that the soul is asleep.

There are, of course, astonishing glimpses of resurrection life in the Old Testament but the texts do not prove that we are conscious between death and the day of resurrection. The best example comes from the prophet Daniel, which could also be seen to support the idea of soul sleep: 'Multitudes who sleep in the dust of the earth will awake: some to everlasting life, others to shame and everlasting contempt' (Dan. 12:2).

Better by far

Coming from the Old Testament into the New is like moving from a darkened room into the sunlight. The apostle Peter tells us that Christ 'was put to death in the body but made alive by the Spirit, through whom also he went and preached to the spirits in prison...' (1 Peter 3:18-19). Whatever view we take of the meaning of these verses, they certainly prove that Christ was conscious after his death. Since this is true of Jesus, why should it not also be true of those who belong to him?

Paul insists that 'to depart and be with Christ is better by far' (Phil. 1:23). The apostle is in two minds – he wants to depart and be with Christ, but at the same time he feels he is still needed by the church. His personal desire however, was to die and enjoy his Master's nearer presence.

Now in what way could Paul enjoy a more intimate union with his Lord if his soul went to sleep? And how could he describe being with Christ in a condition of unconsciousness as being better by far? It is obvious that the apostle never entertained the idea of being unconscious after death. Nor should we.

One more text should be sufficient to prove the point. In argument with the Sadducees who denied the resurrection of the dead, Jesus said: 'But about the resurrection of the dead – have you not read what God said to you, "I am the God of Abraham, the God of Isaac, and the God of Jacob? He is not the God of the dead but of the living"' (Matt. 22:31-32).

Some may argue that a person who is asleep is not dead, but for the living God to establish a living relationship with Abraham, Isaac and Jacob and then terminate it by death (considered as unconsciousness, whether temporary or permanent) is absurd. The word 'dead' in the phrase 'the resurrection of the dead' refers to the raising to life of dead bodies for the purpose of judgment, 'those who have done good will rise to live, and those who have done evil will rise to be condemned' (John 5:29).

Disembodied?

What a horrid word! The thought of the souls of the saints floating around with nothing to replace the human body is most unattractive. The idea of anyone looking forward to such a state stretches the imagination to breaking point. I admit that our understanding of life after death is severely limited, but even so, why would God leave us bereft of a 'house' to live in?

I need no reminding that the body I have occupied for eighty-six years is wearing out and that I must soon abandon it to the worms or the flames. The apostle Paul refers to this body we live in as a tent (2 Cor. 5:1) because he wants to stress its flimsy and temporary nature. Nor do I need reminding that the Lord Jesus Christ is coming again and will re-constitute my disintegrated body and make it like his glorious body. But the thought of being without either, or without some temporary 'tent' to live in does not fill me with joyful expectation.

The fact is, however, that I *am* filled with joyful expectation! Why? Because it is clear to me that the Scriptures hold out the firm hope that after death, in common with all the saints, I shall have a dwelling that is more permanent than a tent. Indeed, it is eternal! Here are the apostle's words: 'Now we know that if the earthly tent we live in is destroyed, we have a building from God, an eternal house in heaven, not built by human hands' (2 Cor. 5:1).

I am fully aware of the alternative ways of understanding Paul's words in the first few verses of 2 Corinthians 5, and I readily admit that it is not an easy passage to understand. Some even conclude that Paul is looking forward to the resurrection body. But the text will not allow such an interpretation. The same is true of all the other suggested alternatives.

The words of Jesus, which teach the same truth, are not difficult to grasp: 'In my Father's house are many rooms; if it were not so, I would have told you' (John 14:2). If you should ask me how the 'eternal house in heaven' fits in with the resurrection body, I would have to say that I have no idea. But this does not disturb me.

Proof that Paul is talking about a body of some kind is to be found in 2 Cor. 5:2-4). Here he changes the metaphor and speaks of being 'clothed with our heavenly dwelling'. From these verses, it is obvious that Paul did not like the idea of being unclothed (or disembodied) either. While we are still in this tent, says the apostle, 'we groan, longing to be clothed with our heavenly dwelling' (verse 2). Every saint should know that this is not pie in the sky. The best is yet to be. We may look forward to unbroken fellowship with the Father and with his Son Jesus Christ through death and into eternity. 'Now it is God who has made us for this very purpose and has given us the Spirit as a deposit, guaranteeing what is to come' (verse 5).